"Jonathan Edwards indisputably is America' is also one of the church's wisest shepherds ᴏ. ᴛʜᴇ Christian soul. In this smart, accessible book, pastor-theologian Sean Lucas shows how Edwards can help us read the story of our salvation as part of the bigger story of God's redemption—what the Father, the Son, and the Holy Spirit have done to rescue us from sin and draw us into the everlasting fellowship of their love."

Philip Graham Ryken, President, Wheaton College; author, *King Solomon: The Temptations of Money, Sex, and Power*

"Those of us trundling through the complete works of Jonathan Edwards in the recent Yale edition are grateful for experts like Sean Lucas who, with a single lucid paragraph, are able to unravel the most complex of Edwardsian thought. The study of Edwards has become something of a 'rite of passage' in recent days, and some of us have some catching up to do. Dr. Lucas, a well-respected Edwards scholar in his own right, has given us a comprehensive summary of Edwards's understanding of the Christian life that does for Edwards what Sinclair Ferguson did for John Owen. An essential and most welcome companion to any serious study of Edwards."

Derek W. H. Thomas, Distinguished Visiting Professor of Systematic and Historical Theology, Reformed Theological Seminary; Minister of Preaching and Teaching, First Presbyterian Church, Columbia, South Carolina; Editorial Director, Alliance of Confessing Evangelicals

"This is an edifying book on a most edifying person, one who became the most important pastor in all of American history. By focusing our attention on what mattered most to Edwards—authentic Christian living that derives from God's grace and reflects God's glory—Sean Lucas has written a book that can draw you nearer to God, even make you a better person. Good theology, well presented, leads to passionate, godly piety. Edwards and Lucas know this well. I pray that you will know it too."

Douglas A. Sweeney, Professor of Church History and the History of Christian Thought, Trinity Evangelical Divinity School; Director, Jonathan Edwards Center

"Sean Michael Lucas analyzes the ways that Jonathan Edwards understood the Christian life as both inconceivably vast and intensely personal and practical, demonstrating that there is still much to be learned from America's greatest philosopher-theologian. From his introduction, to the two invaluable appendices, Lucas offers an eminently useful volume that reminds one of much of Edwards's own writing—technical yet accessible, scholarly yet pastoral."

Richard A. Bailey, Assistant Professor of History, Canisius College; author, *Race and Redemption in Puritan New England*

"It is good for the church—and the heart—to see Sean Lucas, a modern pastor-theologian, working with such depth and clarity in the corpus of Jonathan Edwards, America's preeminent pastor-theologian. Lucas shows a mastery of the vast secondary and primary sources on and by Edwards, yet writes to be understood and to bless the church. If there is a better way to honor the New Light minister, I am not aware of it."

Owen Strachan, coauthor, *The Essential Edwards Collection*; Instructor of Christian Theology and Church History, Boyce College

GOD'S GRAND
DESIGN

GOD'S GRAND DESIGN

THE THEOLOGICAL VISION *of* JONATHAN EDWARDS

SEAN MICHAEL LUCAS

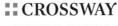
CROSSWAY
WHEATON, ILLINOIS

God's Grand Design: The Theological Vision of Jonathan Edwards
Copyright © 2011 by Sean Michael Lucas
Published by Crossway
          1300 Crescent Street
          Wheaton, Illinois 60187

Cover design: Studio Gearbox
Cover illustration: Allan M. Burch
Interior design and typesetting: Lakeside Design Plus

First printing 2011
Printed in the United States of America

The author's Scripture quotations are from the ESV® Bible (*The Holy Bible, English Standard Version®*), copyright © 2001 by Crossway. Used by permission. All rights reserved.

Trade paperback ISBN:	978-1-4335-1445-6
ePub ISBN:	978-1-4335-2445-5
PDF ISBN:	978-1-4335-1446-3
Mobipocket ISBN:	978-1-4335-1447-0

Library of Congress Cataloging-in-Publication Data
Lucas, Sean Michael, 1970–
    God's grand design : the theological vision of Jonathan Edwards / Sean Michael Lucas.
        p. cm.
    Includes bibliographical references and index.
    ISBN 978-1-4335-1445-6 (tp)
    1. Edwards, Jonathan, 1703–1758. I. Title.
BX7260.E3L83 2011
230'.58—dc23
                                      2011020711

Crossway is a publishing ministry of Good News Publishers.

VP	23	22	21	20	19	18	17	16	15	14	13	12	11
14	13	12	11	10	9	8	7	6	5	4	3	2	1

To S. J. N.
with appreciation

Contents

Contents

Introduction

D uring his lifetime, Jonathan Edwards was many things: pastor, preacher, revivalist, husband, father, author, controversialist. But if he was anything, he was a theologian of the Christian life.

Perhaps this was because, as historian George M. Marsden notes, "he was not a saint by nature. . . . His spiritual life was often an immense struggle. Despite his massive intellect and heroic disciplines, he was, like everyone else, a person with frailties and contradictions." And yet, through his struggles and wrestling with God, Edwards produced a comprehensive theological vision in which he set forth an approach to the Christian life that started with God's glory and ended with all creation returning that glory. It was a vision that remains quite simply magnificent.[1]

And yet, it is a theological vision that has never been adequately explored. Historians and theologians have long argued over whether there was a "center" to Edwards's theology, whether there was an integration point into which all of Edwards's thought fits. Some, like the brilliant Edwards scholar Perry Miller, sought to find a modern Edwards, one that presciently spoke to the needs of a coming age and was martyred in his own. Others, such as theologian John Gerstner, found a rationalist Edwards, one that

---

[1]George M. Marsden, *Jonathan Edwards: A Life* (New Haven, CT: Yale University Press, 2003), 45.

provided theological rigor and rationalist ballast in his approach to his day and our own. Still others, such as historian Michael McClymond and biographer Phillip Gura, appealed to Edwards as the purveyor of religious experience, the ultimate apologetic for yesterday and today. One of the best books on Edwards's theology, still in print, held that he centered his theology in the doctrine of faith. Yet another suggested that God's glory was the beginning point.[2]

All of these attempts to explore Edwards's theology have legitimacy, especially in a day when his thought often seems to be like a "great mirror" in which scholars and readers see their own concerns in his. And yet it is striking that Edwards spent the greatest amount of his time thinking about the Christian life, both for himself and then for his parishioners in his pastoral ministry.[3]

The Christian life certainly was a major preoccupation in his sermons, the regular work in which he engaged from 1726 until his death in 1758. Even a quick perusal of the six published volumes of sermons in *The Works of Jonathan Edwards* edition produced by Yale University Press provides this sense of Edwards's focus. From his earliest sermon, "Christian Happiness," in which he argued that godly people are happy no matter their outward circumstances, Edwards worked the themes of holiness and happiness, seeing and savoring, majesty and meekness, light and darkness—all as representative descriptors of the Christian life. He spoke of the "pleasantness of religion," as well as the way to be "profitable hearers of God's Word," pictured "the true Christian's life [as] a journey towards heaven," delighted in the "excellency

[2]Perry Miller, *Jonathan Edwards* (1949; repr., Amherst: University of Massachusetts, 1981); John Gerstner, *The Rational Biblical Theology of Jonathan Edwards*, 3 vols. (Orlando, FL: Ligonier, 1991); Michael McClymond, *Encounters with God* (New York: Oxford University Press, 1998); Phillip Gura, *Jonathan Edwards: America's Evangelical* (New York: Hill and Wang, 2007); Conrad Cherry, *The Theology of Jonathan Edwards: A Reappraisal* (1966; repr., Bloomington: Indiana University Press, 1990); Stephen Holmes, *God of Grace and God of Glory: An Account of the Theology of Jonathan Edwards* (Grand Rapids: Eerdmans, 2000). For a comprehensive bibliographic overview of books, articles, essays, and dissertations by and about Jonathan Edwards, see M. X. Lesser, *Reading Jonathan Edwards: An Annotated Bibliography in Three Parts, 1729–2005* (Grand Rapids: Eerdmans, 2008).
[3]Peter J. Thuesen, "Jonathan Edwards as Great Mirror," *Scottish Journal of Theology* 50 (1997): 39–60.

of Christ," and urged his people to "renew our Covenant with God." In a variety of ways and in a number of contexts, he sought to inculcate a deep and rich piety among his people.[4]

Edwards did so because it was the major preoccupation of his own life. He would later relate to his son-in-law, Aaron Burr, "I felt in me a burning desire to be in everything a complete Christian; and conformed to the blessed image of Christ: and that I might in all things, according to the pure, sweet, and blessed rules of the gospel." He went on to observe, "It was my continual strife day and night, and constant inquiry, how I should be more holy, and live more holily, and more becoming a child of God, and disciple of Christ." He desired to raise his "religious affections" to a holy ardor through Scripture reading and prayer, attendance upon the means of grace, and encountering the spiritual relations of others.[5]

But Edwards's view of piety was far more than heightened emotions. Rather, he developed a full theology and history of the Christian life, beginning in eternity past with the mutual delight that God had in himself and extending it into the future in which heaven would be a "world of love." By rooting his understanding of God's purposes in his own Trinitarian being, and especially God's passion to glorify himself by communicating his glory in creation and redemption and receiving back his glory in love and praise, Edwards set forth a vision of the Christian life that was deeply *theological*.

---

[4]Jonathan Edwards, "Christian Happiness," in *The Works of Jonathan Edwards* (hereafter *WJE*), vol. 10, *Sermons and Discourses, 1720–1723*, ed. Wilson H. Kimnach (New Haven, CT: Yale University Press, 1992), 296–307; Edwards, "The Pleasantness of Religion" and "Profitable Hearers of the Word," in *WJE*, vol. 14, *Sermons and Discourses, 1723–1729*, ed. Kenneth P. Minkema (New Haven, CT: Yale University Press, 1997), 97–115, 243–77; Edwards, "The True Christian's Life a Journey Towards Heaven," in *WJE*, vol. 17, *Sermons and Discourses, 1730–1733*, ed. Mark Valeri (New Haven, CT: Yale University Press, 1999), 427–46; Edwards, "The Excellency of Christ," in *WJE*, vol. 19, *Sermons and Discourses, 1734–1738*, ed. M. X. Lesser (New Haven, CT: Yale University Press, 2001), 560–94; Edwards, "Renewing Our Covenant with God," in *WJE*, vol. 22, *Sermons and Discourses, 1739–1742*, eds. Harry S. Stout and Nathan O. Hatch, with Kyle Farley (New Haven, CT: Yale University Press, 2003), 509–18.
[5]Jonathan Edwards, "Personal Narrative," in *WJE*, vol. 16, *Letters and Personal Writings*, ed. George S. Claghorn (New Haven, CT: Yale University Press, 1998), 795.

As a result, this book on Edwards's view of the Christian life must be theological as well. The question becomes one of framework: If the Christian life was central to Edwards's theological and pastoral reflection, how did he frame those reflections? I'd suggest that Edwards's framework ran in two directions, or, perhaps better, at two levels. On one level, his theological vision for the Christian life was cosmic: the grand narrative of the history of the work of redemption. Edwards had intended, were he to live longer, to write a theology of the Christian life that would be "divinity in an entire new method." Redemption would be at the center of human history, but that grand work of God would reach back to eternity past and find its fulfillment in eternity future.

Therefore, part 1 of this book focuses on "redemption history." We will follow Edwards back to eternity past, into the very delight the persons of the Trinity had for each other; journey into time by means of God's covenant of redemption with himself to create and purchase a people for his own glory; pay attention to history as God's gracious works of creation and redemption unfold in space and time; watch the unfolding of that work of redemption in time through the successive revivals and reforms of the church; and thrill at the gathering up of all things on earth in heaven.[6]

There was a second level on which Edwards's theological vision operated: the personal. How does this cosmic work of redemption, the "uniting of all things in Christ," get applied to the individual's life so that he or she becomes part of it? Part 2 focuses on "redemption applied": God's grace coming to individuals as a divine and supernatural light, immediately illuminating the mind, stirring the affections, and moving the will; the new sense of the heart and holy affections that lead to new Christian practices; the response of obedient faith that clings to God; the ethics of universal and disinterested benevolence to God and all

---

[6]Jonathan Edwards to the trustees of the College of New Jersey, October 19, 1757, in *WJE*, 16:727; Harry S. Stout, "Jonathan Edwards' Tri-World Vision," in *The Legacy of Jonathan Edwards: American Religion and the Evangelical Tradition*, ed. D. G. Hart, Sean Michael Lucas, and Stephen J. Nichols (Grand Rapids: Baker, 2003), 27–46.

his creatures. What makes Edwards's theology of the Christian life so pastorally and spiritually valuable is not simply the positive theological statement he makes; as a "man like us," he recognized like no one else, save John Calvin, the reality of self-deception and the necessity of continued renewal. His patient description of what the Christian life is *and is not* continues to serve as an important guide for contemporary believers as they seek to live for God's glory. He emphasized the means of grace—the ministry of the Word, sacraments, and prayer—as sustaining food in the wilderness and as means of continued communion with Christ. And his clear-sighted determination to speak to his people in every stage of their Christian journey was part of his desire that everyone reach heaven safely.

To chart these themes well means that at times this book may be rough sledding for some. Having taught on Jonathan Edwards to seminarians, I've walked with them through his knotty passages and complex thoughts; but these require careful thought, precise statement, and sometimes rereading. For others, there will be the temptation to reify Edwards's vision as the standard by which all other approaches must be judged. However, the value of this capacious view of God is not merely in the details, but also in the outlines of a large view of God's grand design. Importantly, Edwards himself recognized this. As he wrote to the College of New Jersey trustees, to unpack his theology of the Christian life in special relationship to the work of redemption was simply to pay attention to "the grand design of all God's designs, and the *summum* and *ultimum* of all the divine operations and degrees." To join Edwards in this big vision of God's glorious work is to strengthen our understanding of what God has called us to be and to do in this world. By God's mercy, such effort is worth it.[7]

---

[7]Jonathan Edwards to the trustees of the College of New Jersey, October 19, 1757, *WJE*, 16:728.

If there was ever a book that had a long gestation period, it is this one. I've been thinking and writing about Jonathan Edwards since my early days in graduate school. As a result, I have a number of people to whom I am indebted and to whom I must express my gratitude. First and foremost, Sara, Sam, Liz, Drew, and Ben Lucas deserve my thanks. Sara has known Jonathan Edwards as long as I have, since our days as college students. While we have a most uncommon union, like Edwards and his Sarah, I cannot imagine my life without my Sara or our children. Thanks as well to my parents, Steve and Susan Lucas, and my parents-in-law, Ron and Phyllis Young; grateful for your love and support.

I'm thankful to Steve Nichols and Crossway's Justin Taylor, who encouraged me to contribute this work. I'm also grateful to the entire team at Crossway, from Al Fisher on, who have made this such a pleasure. Thanks especially to Thom Notaro, whose careful editing made this a much better book. Thanks to my teachers, mentors, and friends in Edwards studies: David Beale, George Claghorn, Sam Logan, Peter Lillback, D. G. Hart, Richard Bailey, Greg Wills, Amy Pauw, Gerald McDermott, Mark Valeri, Michael McClymond, and Doug Sweeney. I'm grateful as well for the Jonathan Edwards Center at Yale University; without their fine online search engine, indexes, and transcriptions (at http://edwards.yale.edu), this project would have been impossible to complete.

This project began while I was a faculty member at Covenant Theological Seminary. I express my gratitude to seminary president Bryan Chapell and the board of trustees for granting me a sabbatical in the spring of 2009 to work on this book. The administration and faculty were hugely supportive of my writing; for that I'm forever grateful. While I taught at Covenant, I worked my way through this material with two sets of students in spring 2005 and fall 2008; thank you, students, for your input, encouragement, and engagement. I also acknowledge the seminary's permission to use "'A Man Just Like Us': Jonathan Edwards and Spiritual Formation for Ministerial Candidates," *Presbyterion* 30, no. 1 (2004): 1–10, and "'Divine Light, Holy

Heat': Jonathan Edwards, the Ministry of the Word, and Spiritual Formation," *Presbyterion* 34 (2008): 1–12. Both appear in this book: the former as an appendix, the latter as the bulk of chapter 9.

A large portion of this book was completed after my transition to serve as senior minister at the First Presbyterian Church, Hattiesburg, Mississippi. I'm grateful to my fellow pastors, ministry staff, and elders, who encouraged me to fulfill my twin calling as pastor and writer, and who provided me extra time to complete this book on time. It is a great joy to serve with you as together we see the grace of the gospel transform us, as well as our city, for his glory. Over the last several weeks of writing, my congregation prayed for me, updated by my tweets and Facebook posts; thank you all. I'm sure you recognize some of the things in this book!

Nearly twenty years ago, when I walked onto the campus of Westminster Theological Seminary, I met a guy, my age, who was working in the bookstore. As we went to seminars together and worked in the back room of the store together, we dreamed of books we would write and made up titles for them. In God's providence, we've gotten to do some of that and even have worked together on one book. We've had Edwards in common the entire time, but even more, a solid friendship. This book and its dedication mark that friendship and the "sweet union and communion" we've enjoyed in Christ.

Part One

REDEMPTION
HISTORY

CHAPTER I

God's Grand Design

The Glory of God

I t had been four years since the glow of revival began to fade in Northampton, Massachusetts. The "surprising work of God" had once again become the hum of the regular works of men and women in their day-to-day lives. As the pastor of the Congregational Church in Northampton and the one responsible for the spiritual condition of these folks, Jonathan Edwards wrestled with how to lead his people to experience once again the spiritual renewal that came through heightened, holy affections.

During this period, Edwards tried to remind his people of their spiritual experiences by publishing accounts of the awakenings for the Anglo-American world. By 1737, *A Faithful Narrative of the Surprising Work of God* had become a key piece of the religious propaganda of the period, serving as both a report of the religious revival and a model of how such renewal might happen in other locations. The following year he also published key sermons from the 1734–1735 awakening, expanding his sermon "Justification by Faith Alone," as well as adding other successful revival sermons.[1]

In addition, Edwards began to experiment with the sermon model. The period from 1734 to 1742 saw his greatest creativity as a preacher. He preached several long series on single texts, leading his congregation to consider 2 Corinthians 13:5, 1 Corinthians 13, Matthew 25:1–12, and 1 Peter 1:8 in multi-unit sermon series. The greatest of these sermonic experiments was his thirty-unit sermon on Isaiah 51:8, preached over six months in 1739, which has come to us as "A History of the Work of Redemption." Historian John Wilson held that these sermons represented "a new and different kind of project" in which Edwards "transformed" the structure of the sermon in order to accomplish his larger purpose.[2]

Edwards's larger purpose was to raise his congregation's vision from its apparently mundane and petty daily concerns to find their affections engaged by the cosmic purpose that God has in his work of redemption. And God's grand design in the work of redemption was nothing less than his own glory.

In all this God designed to accomplish the glory of the blessed Trinity in an exceeding degree. God had a design of glorifying himself from eternity, to glorify each person in the Godhead. The end must be considered as first in the order of nature and

[1]Jonathan Edwards, "A Faithful Narrative of the Surprising Work of God," in *The Works of Jonathan Edwards* (hereafter *WJE*), vol. 4, *The Great Awakening*, ed. C. C. Goen (New Haven, CT: Yale University Press, 1972); Frank Lambert, *Inventing the "Great Awakening"* (Princeton, NJ: Princeton University Press, 2001); Jonathan Edwards, "Justification by Faith Alone," in *WJE*, vol. 19, *Sermons and Discourses, 1734–1738*, ed. M. X. Lesser (New Haven, CT: Yale University Press, 2001).
[2]Jonathan Edwards, "Charity and Its Fruits," in *WJE*, vol. 8, *Ethical Writings*, ed. Paul Ramsey (New Haven, CT: Yale University Press, 1989); Ava Chamberlain, "Brides of Christ and Signs of Grace: Edwards's Sermon Series on the Parable of the Wise and Foolish Virgins," in *Jonathan Edwards's Writings: Text, Context, Interpretation*, ed. Stephen J. Stein (Bloomington: Indiana University Press, 1996), 3–18; John F. Wilson, "Editor's Introduction," in *WJE*, vol. 9, *A History of the Work of Redemption*, ed. John F. Wilson (New Haven, CT: Yale University Press, 1989), 2, 10.

then the means, and therefore we must conceive that God having proposed this end had then, as it were, the means to choose.

Far from focusing on a merely individual salvation, Edwards rooted his understanding of the Christian life in the cosmic purpose of God himself—namely, for God to glorify himself and enjoy himself forever.[3]

Far from wanting an abstract theological construction with little bearing on actual Christian living, Edwards recognized that only as Christians have their vision filled with God's grand purpose to glorify himself through his work of redemption are their affections transformed, their wills moved, and their beings engaged in benevolence toward all creation. Yet in order for believers truly to grasp such a vision, they need to see that God's purpose to glorify himself through creation and redemption is an outflow of his own eternal being.

Trinity

Edwards's theology of the Christian life is profoundly Trinitarian. As he said in his sermons on God's work of redemption, God purposed to glorify each person of the Trinity in his grand design. And yet, God's design was much more expansive than this. Edwards suggests that God's purpose was to draw human beings into God's own glorious life that they might share in and reflect back divine love and glory.[4]

The Psychological Analogy

God's own being as Trinity served as a key building block in Edwards's theological development, and Edwards staked out his position early in his ministry. In an entry in his "Miscellanies,"

---

[3]Jonathan Edwards, "A History of the Work of Redemption," in *WJE*, 9:125; John Piper, *Brothers, We Are Not Professionals: A Plea to Pastors for Radical Ministry* (Nashville: Broadman and Holman, 2002), 6.
[4]The key book on Edwards's Trinitarian theology is Amy Plantinga Pauw, *The Supreme Harmony of All: The Trinitarian Theology of Jonathan Edwards* (Grand Rapids: Eerdmans, 2002); see also, much more densely, William J. Danaher Jr., *The Trinitarian Ethics of Jonathan Edwards* (Louisville: Westminster John Knox, 2004).

written when he was twenty years old, Edwards offered a defense of the Trinity based on the dictates of "naked reason." Drawing from a version of the psychological analogy pioneered by Augustine in the fourth century, Edwards assumed that God exists and that God posits certain ideas about himself. These ideas of himself are unmediated and perfect; God's self-perception serves as a type of perfect mirror or image. Such an image has of necessity always existed since God himself has always existed; just as God had no beginning, this self-reflection had no beginning either. It is "eternally begotten," as it were.[5]

Further, as God contemplates this perfect idea of himself, God naturally delights in this self-reflection. As he sees his perfections, he delights in them; as this has occurred eternally, so God has had eternal and infinite delight in himself. But it is more; since this idea of himself is a perfect reflection of God, this idea returns God's own delight. A cycle of delight passes between God and his image; indeed, infinite love and "an infinitely sweet energy we call delight," which is a pure act, move between God and his idea. And thus, Edwards has "proved" the Trinity: "God, the idea of God, and delight in God."

In this analogy, God the Father contemplates the expressed, eternally begotten, image of himself, God the Son; the delight that eternally processes between them is God the Holy Spirit. Edwards would extend this analogy, but never abandon it. While there are undoubtedly problems with this understanding, it is foundational for his understanding of the being of God within God's self (*ad intra*).[6]

---

[5] Jonathan Edwards, "The 'Miscellanies,' no. 94," in *WJE*, vol. 13, *The "Miscellanies," a–500*, ed. Thomas A. Schafer (New Haven, CT: Yale University Press, 1994), 256–63. The following two paragraphs offer a summary of Edwards's argument.

[6] To name just two problems: (1) This divine contemplation occurs within the mind of God; how do you establish real existence of the Son (idea) and Spirit (delight) outside God's contemplation of them? (2) While the Son (idea) seems to reflect the personality of God, how does the Spirit (delight) have the two key aspects of personality—understanding and will—in this model? Importantly, Edwards himself recognized these problems and sought to address them in "Discourse on the Trinity," in *WJE*, vol. 21, *Writings on the Trinity, Grace, and Faith*, ed. Sang Hyun Lee (New Haven, CT: Yale University Press, 2003), 132–33.

Edwards would replicate this understanding and expand it in a manuscript that he worked on periodically throughout the 1730s. There he would once again argue that

> when we speak of God's happiness, the account that we are wont to give of it is that God is infinitely happy in the enjoyment of himself, in perfectly beholding and infinitely loving, and rejoicing in, his own essence and perfections. And accordingly it must be supposed that God perpetually and eternally has a most perfect idea of himself, as it were an exact image and representation of himself. . . . And from hence arises a most pure and perfect energy in the Godhead, which is the divine love, complacence and joy.

In other words, God's own happiness is at the very center of who God is.[7]

The Social Analogy

But Edwards would also utilize another analogy for understanding the Trinity, the social analogy. A twelfth-century theologian named Richard St. Victor apparently pioneered this understanding in the Western church, although it had a rich history in the Eastern Orthodox Church going back to the Cappadocian fathers. Edwards described the Trinity as a "society or family of the three." All three of the persons in the Godhead have understanding and will, but each exercises his understanding and will in a specific way as part of the divine economy. All three share honor, but each receives a "peculiar honor in the society or family." All three agree in the work of redemption, but each has a specific role in that work and receives honor for that particular role.[8]

And so, from all eternity, God's own inner being was one of utter delight and love among the three. As God enjoyed eternal happiness in himself, receiving glory and honor from himself and returning glory and honor to himself, he was utterly satisfied

[7]Ibid., 21:113.
[8]Ibid., 21:135–36.

in himself. As Edwards noted, "It is evident, by both Scripture and reason, that God is infinitely, eternally, unchangeably, and independently glorious and happy: that he stands in no need of, cannot be profited by, or receive anything from the creature."[9]

Although God was utterly satisfied within his own inner Trinitarian life, the wonder is that he decided to create the earth and populate it with human beings. According to Edwards, God's ultimate purpose in creating the world was

> to communicate of his own infinite fullness of God; or rather it was his last end, that there might be a glorious and abundant emanation of his infinite fullness of good *ad extra*, or without himself, and the disposition to communicate himself or diffuse his own fullness, which we must conceive of as being originally in God as a perfection of his nature, was what moved him to create the world.

Edwards is saying something incredibly profound: God's purpose in creating was to communicate the fullness of Trinitarian delight outside himself.[10]

However, that is not all. God not only desires to communicate (or emanate) the overflow of his goodness and glory, but also desires for that goodness and glory to return (or to be remanated) to himself. This goodness and glory will return to God in the happiness and delight of his creation. In an early "Miscellanies" entry, Edwards observed that the happiness of the saints would be "as transcendent as the glory of God, seeing it is the same." As the saints know the happiness that comes in response to the manifestation of God's glory and excellency, they reflect back to God his own glory. God's fullness is communicated and returned in a never-ending cycle of love.[11]

This was part of the grand benefit that Christ secured for his people through his redemption: that they would be included in this Trinitarian world of happiness and delight. "Christ has

---

[9]Jonathan Edwards, "The End for Which God Created the World," in *WJE*, 8:420.
[10]Ibid., 8:433–34.
[11]"The 'Miscellanies,' no. 106," *WJE*, 13:276–77.

brought it to pass," Edwards noted, "that those that the Father has given him should be brought into the household of God, that he and his Father and they should be as it were one society, one family; that his people should be in a sort admitted into that society of the three persons in the Godhead." Here, then, is the connecting point back to Edwards's sermons on the work of redemption: Christ's redemption accomplishes God's grand design of drawing God's redeemed creation into the Trinitarian life that they might participate and communicate in the eternal happiness of God.[12]

Covenant

This grand design of the triune God—that of drawing redeemed creation into the very life of heaven—is accomplished by means of covenant. Edwards noted this truth in the very first sermon in his series "A History of the Work of Redemption." "There were many things done in order to the Work of Redemption before [the fall]. Some things were done before the world was created, yea from all eternity," he preached. "The persons of the Trinity were as it were confederated in a design and a covenant of redemption, in which the Father appointed the Son and the Son had undertaken their work, and all things to be accomplished in their work were stipulated and agreed." In order to accomplish his purpose of glorifying himself, God established a covenant.[13]

In Edwards's understanding, the covenantal structure of God's dealing with human beings involves the covenants of redemption, works, and grace.

The Covenant of Redemption

As the language from "A History of the Work of Redemption" demonstrates, Edwards's understanding of the covenant of redemption had two elements: it was pretemporal and it was

[12]Jonathan Edwards, "The 'Miscellanies,' no. 570," in *WJE*, vol. 18, *The "Miscellanies," 501–832*, ed. Ava Chamberlain (New Haven, CT: Yale University Press, 2000), 110.
[13]"A History of the Work of Redemption," *WJE*, 9:118.

intra-Trinitarian. Edwards held that Christ covenanted with the other two members of the Godhead before the foundation of the world to purchase the salvation of the elect, and in so doing to glorify God himself.

The Covenant of Works

Edwards also developed a thorough understanding of a prelapsarian (i.e., prefall) covenant of works. God made a covenant with Adam, who stood as a representative of his posterity. Edwards wrote,

> It must appear to every impartial person, that Moses' account does, with sufficient evidence, lead all mankind, to whom this account is communicated, to understand that God, in constitution [covenant] with Adam, dealt with him as a public person, and as the head of the human species, and had respect to his posterity as included in him.

Adam stood as a forefather and representative for all humanity.[14]

In establishing this covenant, God required perfect obedience from Adam. If Adam had satisfied the divine demand, he would have received reward: "If Adam had stood and persevered in obedience, he would have been made happy by mere bounty and goodness; for God was not obliged to reward Adam for his perfect obedience any otherwise than by covenant, for Adam by standing would not have merited happiness." Adam would not have received reward solely for merit; rather, God would grant "reward" because he chose to make covenant with Adam and to require certain conditions. In other words, the ground of reward was God's own free promise; the condition was obedience.[15]

Even more, if Adam had obeyed, his posterity would have received the blessing of eternal life. "If Adam had stood and got the victory, all his posterity would have had a right to the

---

[14]Jonathan Edwards, *WJE*, vol. 3, *Original Sin*, ed. Clyde A. Holbrook (New Haven, CT: Yale University Press, 1970), 260.
[15]Jonathan Edwards, "Glorious Grace," in *WJE*, vol. 10, *Sermons and Discourses, 1720–1723*, ed. Wilson H. Kimnach (New Haven, CT: Yale University Press, 1992), 392.

reward without another trial," Edwards held. "The first Adam was to have performed the condition of life; his posterity were not properly to perform any condition." All that Adam's posterity would have needed to do to enjoy reward was to be born. Adam would have been invited to eat from the tree of life "as a seal of his reward." Death would have been "put out of all possibility" for Adam and his posterity. "He now enjoyed life, but if he had stood he would have been called to the tree of life to eat of that, and his life should not only have been ascertained to him forever, but he would have advanced to a higher degree of life" and a "much greater happiness."[16]

Although Adam did not obey, the covenant of works was not abrogated. Instead, it remains as an eternal and immutable covenant with its demands against humankind in full force. Edwards suggested that "if we speak of the covenant God has made with man stating the condition of eternal life, God never made but one with man, to wit, the covenant of works; which never yet was abrogated but is a covenant [that] stands in full force to all eternity without the failing of one tittle."[17] In Edwards's estimation, the one covenant that God has made with humankind is not one of grace, but one of works. God's requirement for humankind throughout history is the same as for Adam in the garden, namely, perfect obedience.

This requirement for humankind was restated in the Ten Commandments. Edwards equivocated a bit on whether the Ten Commandments served as a restatement of the covenant of works or as a rule of life for believers. On the one hand, "the covenant of works was here [in the Ten Commandments] exhibited to be as a schoolmaster to lead to Christ, not only for the use of that nation in the ages of the Old Testament, but for the use of God's church throughout all ages to the end of the world." God's demand for perfect obedience is restated in the moral law; the threatening of

[16]"The 'Miscellanies,' no. 171," *WJE*, 13:324; Jonathan Edwards, "East of Eden," in *WJE*, vol. 17, *Sermons and Discourses, 1730–1733*, ed. Mark Valeri (New Haven, CT: Yale University Press, 1999), 332, 337.
[17]"The 'Miscellanies,' no. 30," *WJE*, 13:217.

future judgment for the failure of obedience is brought to bear; and the longing for a Redeemer who could satisfy God's wrath and fulfill the law's demand is created.[18]

On the other hand, "if we regard this law now given at Mount Sinai not as a covenant of works but as a rule of life, so it is made use [of] by the Redeemer from that time to the end of the world as a directory to his people, to show them the way in which they must walk, as they would go to heaven." The Ten Commandments then serve as a rule of life to guide the regenerate in the life that pleases God. The law drives men and women to Jesus; and Jesus drives men and women back to the law.[19]

The Covenant of Grace

However the Ten Commandments are understood, the fact is that the continuing demand of the covenant of works remains a major problem for humankind. Because of Adam's fall, his posterity was plunged into a condition of sin and misery. Original righteousness was lost; corruption came to characterize every thought, word, and deed. Perfect and perpetual obedience became impossible. And so, God in his mercy sent Jesus as the new mediator of the covenant, the covenant of grace. But for Edwards, the covenant of grace is not different from the covenant of works; rather, he holds the two together: "The covenant of grace is not another covenant made with man upon the abrogation of [the covenant of works], but a covenant made with Christ to fulfill [the covenant of works]. And for this end came Christ into the world, to fulfill the law, or covenant of works, for all that receive him." There are not really two covenants, but one, and the covenant of works becomes the covenant of grace for those who trust in Jesus.[20]

Jesus came as the great mediator, the true Adam, to fulfill all that the first Adam failed to do and to satisfy all that the covenant

[18]"A History of the Work of Redemption," *WJE*, 9:180.
[19]Ibid., 9:181.
[20]"The 'Miscellanies,' no. 30," *WJE*, 13:217.

of works demanded. As Edwards preached in "A History of the Work of Redemption" sermons:

> Every command that Christ obeyed may be reduced to that great and everlasting law of God that is contained in the covenant of works, that eternal rule of righteousness that God had established between himself and mankind. Christ came into the world to fulfill and answer the covenant of works, that is the covenant that is to stand forever as a rule of judgment, and that is the covenant that we had broken, and that was the covenant that must be fulfilled.

In the covenant of grace, Jesus fulfills the covenant of works and sets believers free from its demands and condemnation.[21]

So the covenant of grace is an absolute promise to those who believe in Jesus.[22] By "absolute promise," Edwards meant that a person's ability to meet the covenant conditions is given by God; as a result, God is the one ultimately who made and satisfies the covenant. God made the covenant with Jesus and all the elect in him from the foundation of the world; he sent Jesus to satisfy the demands of the covenant of works through his own obedience and death; and he supplies faith and evangelical obedience to all the elect that they might trust in him. From beginning to the end, the covenant of grace relies on God's grace.

> There is nothing wanting but our willing and hearty reception of Christ, yet we shall eternally perish yet, if God is not gracious to us, and don't make application of Christ's benefits to our souls. We are dependent on free grace, even for ability to lay hold on Christ already offered so entirely is the gospel dispensation of mere grace. That is, we shall be saved freely and for nothing if we will but accept of Christ, but we are not able to do that of ourselves, but it is the free gift of God.

---

[21] "A History of the Work of Redemption," *WJE*, 9:308–9.

[22] "The new covenant as a mutual agreement, or as a conditional promise, is only with Christ; but as 'covenant' sometimes signifies an absolute promise, so it is with believers, and with none other of mankind that those that actually believe." "The 'Miscellanies,' no. 165," *WJE*, 13:321.

As a result, God's covenant of grace is absolute; God will fully accomplish the salvation of the elect.[23]

The covenant of grace is also binding, both for God and for his people. Edwards suggested that God "condescended to become bound to us by covenant." In fact, God relinquishes "his absolute freedom and should cease to be merely sovereign in his dispensations toward believers when once they have believed in Christ, and should, for their more abundant consolation, become bound." As a result, human beings can "challenge salvation of this Sovereign; they can demand it of Christ as a debt." And God will supply his grace because he "bound himself by his oath" to do so.[24]

Human beings are bound to fulfill the terms of the covenant: faith and evangelical obedience. Edwards believed that humans comply with the binding terms of the covenant of grace when they believe in Jesus. He claimed that

> there is an act of choice or election in true and saving faith, whereby the soul chooses Christ for its Savior, and accepts and embraces him as such. . . . Faith is a duty, which God requires of it. We are commanded to believe and unbelief is a sin forbidden of God. Faith is a duty required in the first table of the law and in the first commandment of it.

In order to gain any benefit from God's covenant, "there is a certain condition [that] must be performed by us. We must believe in the Lord Jesus Christ, and accept of him as offered in the gospel for a Savior." And yet, Edwards also recognized that people in

---

[23] "Glorious Grace," *WJE*, 10:394–95.
[24] Jonathan Edwards, "God's Sovereignty in Salvation of Men," in *The Works of Jonathan Edwards*, ed. Edward Hickman, 2 vols. (1834; repr., Carlisle, PA: Banner of Truth, 1974), 2:854. Elsewhere Edwards wrote, "Salvation is an absolute debt to the believer from God, so that he may in justice demand it, on account of what his surety has done. For Christ has satisfied justice fully for his sin; so that it is but a thing that may be challenged, that God should now release the believer from the punishment; it is but a piece of justice that the creditor should release the debtor, when he has fully paid the debt. And again, the believer may demand eternal life, but it has been merited by Christ, by a merit of condignity. So is it contrived, that that justice that seemed to require man's destruction, now requires his salvation." Edwards, "Wisdom of God Displayed in the Way of Salvation," in Hickman, *The Works of Jonathan Edwards*, 2:148.

themselves cannot believe; Christ purchased this gift for all the elect: "He has purchased, that they shall have faith given them; whereby they shall be [actively] united to Christ, and so have a [pleadable] title to his benefits."[25]

Edwards favored marital imagery when talking about how God and humans are mutually bound to each other in the covenant of grace. Both husband and wife pledge to fulfill certain responsibilities in marriage. In the same way, God and humans both fulfill certain responsibilities in order to be in covenant with one another. "Love desires that the right be mutual," Edwards observed.

> The lover desires, not only to have a right to the beloved, but that the beloved should also have a right to him. Provision is also made for this, in this wise method of salvation, that God should have a special propriety in the redeemed, that they should be in a distinguishing manner his, that they should be his peculiar people.

Hence, in the covenant, the believer has the right to claim the blessings of God, as summed up in the divine promise, "I will be your God." Not only do we have a "claim" upon God; he also has a claim upon his people that they should be his "peculiar people." God derives enjoyment from his people as he basks in the light of their delight, love, and praise.[26]

Trinitarian Purpose

What we cannot and must not miss is that the whole focus of God's covenant promise to gain a people for himself through Jesus Christ is his own glory. When all human history is completed and all of God's covenantal purposes are accomplished in this work of redemption, the triune God will be perfectly glorified: "And now shall Christ the great Redeemer be most perfectly glorified, and God the Father shall be glorified in him, and the

[25]"Charity and Its Fruits," *WJE*, 8:139–40; "Wisdom of God," 146–47.
[26]On marital imagery, see for example, Jonathan Edwards, "An Humble Inquiry," in *WJE*, vol. 12, *Ecclesiastical Writings*, ed. David D. Hall (New Haven, CT: Yale University Press, 1994), 205–7; "Wisdom of God," 146.

Holy Ghost shall [be] most fully glorified in the perfection of his work in the hearts of all the church." The grand design of God will be completed at the end of the age when all of his decrees are accomplished, his covenant is fulfilled, and his glory, wisdom, and power are on full display in the saints of God.[27]

Far from developing a dry theological schema, Edwards believed that pointing his people to the Trinity's covenantal purpose would inflame their hearts and draw out their praise. After all, in tracing the history of God's redemptive work, "we see where it issues: as it began in God, so it ends in God. God is the infinite ocean into which it empties itself." And because the entirety of human history starts and ends with the triune God, the people of God should orient their entire beings to this eschatological and doxological purpose.[28]

---

[27]"A History of the Work of Redemption," *WJE*, 9:509; Edwards specifically mentions God's glory, wisdom, and power on pp. 522–25.
[28]Ibid., 9:519.

CHAPTER 2

God's End in Creating the World

Creation, Nature, Fall

The most striking thing about Jonathan Edwards's sermon series "A History of the Work of Redemption" is that in his desire to present "divinity in an entire new method"— a method that we now would call "redemptive-historical"—he slighted the importance of God's work of creation. That is illustrated most forcibly in the very structure of the sermon itself, which starts with the fall of Adam.[1]

The upshot of this theological and homiletical decision is that God's works of creation and redemption are separated; creation is viewed as somewhat incidental and subservient to the more significant work of redemption. And, in fact, Edwards frequently

---

[1] Jonathan Edwards to the trustees of the College of New Jersey, October 19, 1757, in *The Works of Jonathan Edwards* (hereafter *WJE*), vol. 16, *Letters and Personal Writings*, ed. George S. Claghorn (New Haven, CT: Yale University Press, 1998), 727.

spoke of the creation in just these terms. For example, in his "Miscellanies," he notes that "God created the world to glorify himself; but it was principally that he might glorify him[self] in his disposal of the world, or in the use he intended to make of it, in his providence." And the work that God intended to make of creation was the work of redemption.

> All other works of providence may be looked upon as *appendages* to this great work, or *things* which God does to subserve that grand design. The work of redemption may be looked upon as the great end and drift of all God's works and dispensations from the beginning, and even the end of the work of creation itself; yea, the whole creation.

Redemption is the grand design of God; creation is but the stage on which that drama plays.[2]

Although Edwards related creation and redemption after this manner, it is somewhat surprising—if for no other reason than that Edwards himself prized creation and nature as highly as any Christian of his day and thought theologically about creation as thoroughly as any theologian of his or any other time. Edwards viewed creation and nature as a window to view God's glory and as a means to raise holy affections: "Indeed the whole outward creation, which is but the shadows of beings, is so made as to represent spiritual things." Creation serves best when it points beyond itself to redemption; and the believer's task is to see the spiritual in the material and so raise his eyes to heavenly truths.[3]

Though creation and nature could and did function in this way, the fall of Adam, the first and representative human being, plunged the world in general and humankind in particular into a condition of sin and misery. Original righteousness was lost, guilt and corruption pervaded humankind, and God's judgment was justly deserved. But even human sin fit within God's ultimate

---

[2]Jonathan Edwards, "The 'Miscellanies,' no. 702," in *WJE*, vol. 18, *The "Miscellanies," 501–832*, ed. Ava Chamberlain (New Haven, CT: Yale University Press, 2000), 284.
[3]Jonathan Edwards, "The 'Miscellanies,' no. 362," in *WJE*, vol. 13, *The "Miscellanies," a–500*, ed. Thomas A. Schafer (New Haven, CT: Yale University Press, 1994), 434.

end for creating the world. Creation itself serves as the stage in which God gains great glory for himself in redeeming human beings through the mediator, Jesus Christ. Even more, creation will be swallowed up into heaven itself so that Christ will be all and in all.

Creation

Edwards himself experienced great delight in God's creation. As a young man, he would walk in the woods near his parents' home in East Windsor, Connecticut, overwhelmed by God's glory displayed in his world. As an older minister reflecting back on those days, Edwards wrote:

> As I was walking there, and looked upon the sky and clouds; there came into my mind, a sweet sense of the glorious majesty and grace of God, that I know not how to express. I seemed to see them both in a sweet conjunction: majesty and meekness joined together: it was a sweet and gentle, and holy majesty; and also a majestic meekness; an awful sweetness; a high and great and holy gentleness.

God was revealed in his creation; he shined in all that was fair.[4]

Edwards would repeatedly emphasize God's general revelation in his creation, as will be noted below. The theological reason was that creation is, in fact, *God's* creation. Like many Bible interpreters, Edwards held that the form of God's name in Genesis 1:1, being plural, signifies that "the three persons of the Trinity confederated together as to the grand scheme and design of the creation, as they are in the eternal covenant of redemption." At the very beginning of time, the triune God was involved in creating this world and was intent in making this world a fitting stage for his glory.[5]

And yet, the original creation was "a world of confusion and emptiness, full of evil, vanity of vanities." Reflecting the sense of

---

[4]Jonathan Edwards, "Personal Narrative," in *WJE*, 16:793.
[5]Jonathan Edwards, "Genesis 1:1," in *WJE*, vol. 24, *The Blank Bible*, ed. Stephen J. Stein (New Haven, CT: Yale University Press, 2006), 123.

Genesis 1:2 ("the earth was without form and void"), Edwards saw the world as being ordered by God in the rest of the creation account. As the Spirit of God "incubated" creation, he set to work "animating, quickening, adorning, replenishing, and blessing all things." The Spirit gave "form and life and perfection to this empty void and unformed mass." All the fullness of creation was the work of God's own Spirit.[6]

But the height of God's creation was the making of humankind. Once again, Genesis 1 signals that the Trinity was involved in creating: when the text says, "Let us make man," it represents

> a consultation of the persons of the Trinity about the creation of man, for every person had his particular and distinct concern in it, as well as in the redemption of man. The Father employed the Son and the Holy Ghost in this work. The Son endued man with understanding and reason. The Holy Ghost endued him with a holy will and inclination, with original righteousness.

And the triune God blessed the newly created Adam as the "public head of mankind." God granted Adam human society, divine blessing, spiritual good, possession of the earth, and enjoyment in that world. All of this, summed in the "covenant of works" or "covenant of life" made with Adam, was a gift given by God at the very creation of all things.[7]

God not only made this world and its creatures, but also continues to be involved with his creation. Jesus, the Son of God, was the mediator of creation, but he also mediates God's power to uphold the creation. "'Tis evident that the same word, the same Son of God, that made the world or gave it being, also upholds it in being and governs it," Edwards said.

> For 'tis manifest that upholding the world in being is the same with a continued creation, and consequently that creating of

---

[6]Jonathan Edwards, "Notes on Scripture, no. 342," in *WJE*, vol. 15, *Notes on Scripture*, ed. Stephen J. Stein (New Haven, CT: Yale University Press, 1998), 326; "Notes on Scripture, no. 448," *WJE*, 15:530.
[7]Jonathan Edwards, "Genesis 1:26," in *WJE*, 24:126; "Notes on Scripture, no. 398," *WJE*, 15:395.

the world is but the beginning of upholding of it, if I may so
say, the beginning to give the world a supported and dependent
existence; and preservation is only continuing to give it such
a supported existence.

God continues to preserve his world, upholding, governing, and
caring for all his creatures.[8]

Reading Nature's Book

On the surface, this appears to be a fairly straightforward account
of the creation of the world. Though Edwards was not preoc-
cupied with some of the issues that concern contemporary evangelicals (such as the length of creation days), he affirmed that
God made the world out of nothing in the span of six days, made
Adam as the representative head of humankind, and continues
to govern his creation. But why has God done all of this? What
was God's purpose in making this world?

Edwards was very forthright on this point: "It is manifest
that the Scriptures speak, on all occasions, as though God made
himself his end in all his works: and as though the same Being,
who is the first cause of all things, were the supreme and last end
of all things." God made all things for his own glory; as Romans
11:36 puts it, "For from him and through him and to him are all
things. To him be glory forever. Amen."[9]

And so it is that all intelligent creation must and should fall
in with the purpose for which it was created. In this regard, both
general revelation (creation) and special revelation (Scripture)
agree. "Therefore, we justly infer," Edwards reasoned, "that
the same thing which God's revealed law requires intelligent
creatures to seek as their last and greatest end, that God their
Creator has made their last need, and so the end of the creation
of the world." All creation must seek God's glory; that is the

[8]Jonathan Edwards, "The 'Miscellanies,' no. 1358," in *WJE*, vol. 23, *The "Miscellanies,"*
1153–60, ed. Douglas A. Sweeney (New Haven, CT: Yale University Press, 2004), 608.
[9]Jonathan Edwards, "The End for Which God Created the World," in *WJE*, vol. 8,
Ethical Writings, ed. Paul Ramsey (New Haven, CT: Yale University Press, 1989), 467.

purpose for which it was made, to reflect back God's glory to himself.[10]

Because the end of creation is to reflect God's glory back to him, it is not surprising that Edwards sought to read creation itself for signs of God's excellency, beauty, and glory. In order to assist him in these reflections, Edwards put together a notebook that he entitled "Images of Divine Things." In the notebook, he draws parallels between things he saw in God's world and truths found in Scripture. Early in the notebook, he commented on his method.

> It is apparent and allowed that there is a great and remarkable analogy in God's works. There is a wonderful resemblance in the effects which God produces, and consentaneity in his manner of working in one thing and another, throughout all nature. It is very observable in the visible world. Therefore 'tis allowed that God does purposely make and order one thing to be in an agreeableness and harmony with another. . . . We see that even in the material world God makes one part of it strangely to agree with another; and why is it not reasonable to suppose that he makes the whole as a shadow of the spiritual world?[11]

Edwards therefore mined the natural world for signs or types of the spiritual. Roses and thorns signify "that all temporal sweets are mixed with bitter," but even more that "the crown of glory" can come only "by bearing Christ's cross by a life of mortification, self-denial, and labor, and bearing all things for Christ." The ways snakes are able to charm birds in order to kill them "are lively representations of the devil's catching our souls by his temptations." The silkworm stands as a type of Christ in this way: "when it dies, [it] yields us that of which we make such glorious clothing. Christ became a worm for our sakes, and by his death finished that righteousness with which believers are clothed."

---

[10]Jonathan Edwards, "Images of Divine Things, no. 8," in *WJE*, vol. 11, *Typological Writings*, ed. Wallace E. Anderson and Mason I. Lowance Jr., with David Watters (New Haven, CT: Yale University Press, 1993), 53. See also "The End for Which God Created the World," *WJE*, 8:473.

[11]"Images of Divine Things, no. 8," *WJE*, 11:53; see also "The 'Miscellanies,' no. 362," *WJE*, 13:434.

The waves of the ocean during a storm "have a representation of the terrible wrath of God and amazing misery of them that endure it." Lightning commonly strikes high mountains, spires, trees, and the like; this signifies "that heaven is an enemy to all proud persons, and that especially makes such the marks of his vengeance." Moreover, thunder and clouds "have a shadow of the majesty of God." Sun, moon, stars, clouds, and rainbows are all filled with holy meaning and are meant to be read.[12]

Not only is it possible to read nature's book, but it is also possible to read the natural ways of life in this world, established by God, for spiritual benefit. Edwards particularly saw marriage as filled with spiritual meaning. After all, marriage was described as a great mystery in Ephesians 5:32: "By 'mystery' can be meant nothing but a type of what is spiritual." Thus, marriage stands as a sign of "the spiritual union and communion of Christ and the church, and especially the glorification of the church in the perfection of this union and communion forever."[13]

Likewise, meditating on childbirth holds possibility for spiritual benefit. "Children's coming into the world naked and filthy, and in their blood, and crying and impotent," Edwards thought, "is to signify the spiritual nakedness, pollution of nature and wretchedness of condition with which they are born." When children emerge from the womb and cry out, such teaches that all humans are "born to sorrow." And the travails of mothers in labor are significant as well. These represent "the great persecutions and sufferings of the church in bringing forth Christ and in increasing the number of his children; and a type of those spiritual pains that are in the soul when bringing forth Christ."[14]

Even the human body can teach about spiritual things. Human life is sustained by breath to teach "the continual influence of the

---

[12]"Images of Divine Things, no. 3," *WJE*, 11:52; "Images of Divine Things, no. 11," *WJE*, 11:54; "Images of Divine Things, no. 35," *WJE*, 11:59; "Images of Divine Things, no. 27," *WJE*, 11:58; "Images of Divine Things, no. 74," *WJE*, 11:76; "Images of Divine Things, no. 28," *WJE*, 11:58.
[13]"Images of Divine Things, no. 12," *WJE*, 11:54; "Images of Divine Things, no. 5," *WJE*, 11:52.
[14]"Images of Divine Things, no. 10," *WJE*, 11:54; "Images of Divine Things, no. 25," *WJE*, 11:57; "Images of Divine Things, no. 18," *WJE*, 11:55.

Spirit of God that maintains the life of the soul." The pumping of blood from the heart should cause us to see that "out of the heart are the issues of life." Our heads serve as the seat of the soul, though our souls are part of our entire bodies; in the same way "the Godhead dwells in the man Christ Jesus bodily" and "dwells also in believers, by way of participation with the Head." As Edwards read the book of nature, he saw the work of the triune God. He turned his heart to the great end for which God created the world, God's own glory. And his delight in that God increased.[15]

Fall

Though creation was created "very good" and served as a mirror of God's glory, the first human being plunged all of creation into a condition of sin, misery, death, and decay. By virtue of God's "covenant of works," Adam stood as "the head of the whole body and the root of the whole tree." He was a representative head acting on behalf of his posterity; he was also organically connected to them as a tree is with its branches. Because Adam experienced the fall, human beings sinned all.[16]

When Adam was originally created, he was placed in the garden of Eden for a probationary period. At the end of that time, if he had obeyed God's demand for obedience, he would have enjoyed the permanent status of holiness and happiness, eternal life itself. In an early sermon preached during his New York pastorate, Edwards declared, as noted above, that "if Adam had stood and persevered in obedience, he would have been made happy by mere bounty and goodness; for God was not obliged to reward Adam for his perfect obedience any otherwise than by covenant, for Adam by standing would not have merited happiness." Toward the end of his life, writing in his treatise on *Original Sin*, Edwards made the same argument: "Adam, for his persevering obedience, was to have had everlasting life and happiness, in perfect holiness, union

---

[15]"Images of Divine Things, no. 17," *WJE*, 11:55; "Images of Divine Things, no. 6," *WJE*, 11:53; "Images of Divine Things, no. 24," *WJE*, 11:57.
[16]Jonathan Edwards, *WJE*, vol. 3, *Original Sin*, ed. Clyde A. Holbrook (New Haven, CT: Yale University Press, 1970), 389.

with his Maker, and enjoyment of his favor, and this was the life which was to be confirmed by the tree of life."[17]

Adam had some hope of complying with God's requirement of perfect and perpetual obedience because he possessed original righteousness. Adam had the "great rule of righteousness written in his heart" to which God's positive command not to eat of the tree of the knowledge of good and evil corresponded. Even more, in his innocence, Adam had the Holy Spirit as the Spirit of God. In fact, Adam was created with two principles: one was an inferior, natural principle called self-love, which consisted of "those natural appetites and passions which belong to the nature of man, in which his love to his own liberty, honor, and pleasure, were exercises." The Bible calls this natural principle "the flesh." The other principle was a superior, supernatural principle "wherein consisted the spiritual image of God, and man's righteousness and true holiness." The Bible calls this "the divine nature." Both of these principles were in Adam's heart.[18]

Although Adam knew communion with God, was morally innocent, and possessed original righteousness, he still disobeyed God and committed "original sin." The result of our forefather's first sin was "a fatal catastrophe." Edwards speculated that "Adam and Eve immediately lost the beauty and that kind of luster that was on their bodies as soon as they had sinned." They saw each other's nakedness and filthiness and were ashamed. Also, Adam and Eve died that day. "His nature was ruined, the nature of his soul, which ruin is called death in Scripture. . . . The nature of his body was ruined that day, and became mortal, began to die. His whole man became subject to condemnation to death. He was guilty of death."[19]

---

[17]Jonathan Edwards, "Glorious Grace," in *WJE*, vol. 10, *Sermons and Discourses, 1720–1723*, ed. Wilson H. Kimnach (New Haven, CT: Yale University Press, 1992), 392; *Original Sin*, *WJE*, 3:238. See also Jonathan Edwards, "The 'Miscellanies,' no. 884," in *WJE*, vol. 20, *The "Miscellanies," 833–1152*, ed. Amy Plantinga Pauw (New Haven, CT: Yale University Press, 2002), 139–45.

[18]*Original Sin*, *WJE*, 3:381; "The 'Miscellanies,' no. 884," *WJE*, 20:143; "The 'Miscellanies,' no. 894," *WJE*, 20:153; "The 'Miscellanies,' no. 301," *WJE*, 13:387–89. Edwards credited his understanding of original righteousness to his grandfather, Solomon Stoddard.

[19]Jonathan Edwards, "Genesis 3:7," in *WJE*, 24:136–37; "Notes on Scripture, no. 320," *WJE*, 15:302.

Part of Adam's dying was the withdrawal of God's Spirit; as a result, all that remained was "self-love." The effects were thoroughgoing: man "set up himself, and the objects of his private affections and appetites, as supreme; and so they took the place of God." Hence, depravity is not a "new principle" inserted into the soul by God so much as it is the removal of the divine regulation of self-love. "It were easy to shew, how every lust and depraved disposition of man's heart would naturally arise from this *privative* original," Edwards observed.

> Thus 'tis easy to give an account how total corruption of heart should follow on man's eating the forbidden fruit, though that was but one act of sin, *without God's putting* any evil into his heart, or *implanting* any bad principle, or *infusing* any corrupt taint, and so becoming the *author* of depravity.[20]

Adam's corruption, brought about by his sin and God's removal of divine regulation, was transmitted and imputed to his posterity. That is ultimately how Edwards defines original sin.

> By original sin, as the phrase has been most commonly used by divines, is meant the innate sinful depravity of the heart. But yet when the doctrine of original sin is spoken of, it is vulgarly understood in that latitude, as to include not only the depravity of nature, but the imputation of Adam's first sin; or in other words, the liableness or exposedness of Adam's posterity, in the divine judgment, to partake of the punishment of that sin.

Both corruption and imputation of Adam's sin are included in Edwards's understanding.[21]

Imputation—the accounting and transfer of Adam's guilt and corruption to his posterity—happens because God viewed Adam as a representative head for all humankind. As we saw in the previous chapter, Edwards claimed,

---

[20]*Original Sin*, WJE, 3:382, 383.
[21]Ibid., 3:107.

I can't but think it must appear to every impartial person, that Moses' account does, with sufficient evidence, lead all mankind, to whom his account is communicated, to understand that God, in his constitution [covenant] with Adam, dealt with him as a public person, and as the head of the human species, and had respect to his posterity as included him . . . to exhibit to our view the origin of the present sinful miserable state of mankind.

God views all humanity as included in Adam and credits Adam's sin to them.[22]

In order to substantiate that claim, Edwards held that Romans 5 teaches that "all, both Jews and Gentiles, are the posterity of one first father, and all fell in him, and came under condemnation alike by Adam's transgression." This is evidenced in the fact that all human beings die, thus receiving the wages of Adam's sin, whether or not they personally violated Adam's law themselves by their own sin. Of course, the reality is that because of self-love unregulated by the Holy Spirit, all human beings after Adam and Eve inevitably choose what their highest good is, which means their wills are determined to sin.[23]

And sin pervades the entire being of human nature. Indeed, total depravity does not mean that someone is as wicked as they could be; rather it means that he or she is sinful through and through. Edwards put it this way in an early sermon: "The wicked man serves sin with his soul. The sinner serves this master with his whole heart and soul, and all that is within him. His understanding is given up to the obedience of sin; [he] won't see the truth of the plainest thing in the world because sin bids him shut his eyes." Even more importantly, "the will and affections are given up to sin. The sinner wills those things which are agreeable to sin and avoids everything that is contrary thereto." And the sinner's body itself is enslaved to sin as well; everything that the wicked man does is in the service of sin. Edwards's conclusion sums it up: "Thus sin governs the whole man, both soul and body, and

---

[22]Ibid., 3:260.
[23]Jonathan Edwards, "Romans 5:12," in *WJE*, 24:998; "Romans 5:13–14," *WJE*, 24:998–99. See also Edwards's explanation of Romans 5 in *Original Sin*, *WJE*, 3:306–49.

all the actions of both." Every aspect of the human condition knows the corruption of sin.[24]

Because humans participate in Adam's sin and know Adam's corruption, they also experience Adam's judgment, which is death, both physical and eternal. In one 1731 sermon, Edwards observed that "if we had fulfilled the conditions of the first covenant, we should, by what we did, have obtained eternal life and blessedness." But since we did not, the result is judgment: "We had by the fall so incurred God's displeasure." But this is more than displeasure: this is deep and profound divine anger. "The anger of God against all sin is such that it burns to the lowest hell. God has an implacable hatred of sin," Edwards declared. This anger made God an enemy of humankind because "he was angry with him with a displeasure infinitely dreadful, an anger that would surely appear in punishment." And this punishment is eternal death, for Adam and all his posterity.[25]

Yet, even after the fall, God does not abandon either his world or his creatures. "'Tis evident that God is not negligent of the world that he has made. He has made it for his use and, therefore, doubtless he uses it, which implies that he takes care of it and orders and governs it, that it may be directed to the ends for which he has made it," Edwards said later in his life. The ultimate end that God had for creating the world was glory—the communication of his glory to his creation and the reflection of that glory back to God's own self. But in order for that to happen, humankind needed to be rescued, ransomed, restored: in a word, redeemed. The stage of creation was set for the "great work of providence, the work of redemption by Jesus Christ."[26]

---

[24]Jonathan Edwards, "Wicked Man's Slavery to Sin," in *WJE*, 10:343–44. While *Original Sin* is an important source for Edwards's thinking on the fall, another important place where he worked out his understanding was in a sermon on Genesis 3:11, preached in February 1739: Jonathan Edwards, "Sermon on Gen. 3:11," in *WJE Online*, vol. 54, *Sermons, Series II, 1739* (Jonathan Edwards Center at Yale University, 2008).
[25]Jonathan Edwards, "East of Eden," in *WJE*, vol. 17, *Sermons and Discourses, 1730–1733*, ed. Mark Valeri (New Haven, CT: Yale University Press, 1999), 337, 339, 340.
[26]"The 'Miscellanies,' no. 1304," *WJE*, 23:255; "The End for Which God Created the World," *WJE*, 8:485.

CHAPTER 3

The Great Errand of Christ

Redemption

The centerpiece of Edwards's thirty-unit sermon "A History of the Work of Redemption" was the work of Jesus on the cross. Of course, that was fitting in more ways than one. It was fitting because the center of the Christian faith is the crucifixion and resurrection of Jesus: his once-for-all, bloody sacrifice on the cross placated the wrath of God against the elect, and his resurrection from the dead vindicated Jesus as the Son of God.

It was fitting as well because the events of redemption serve as the hinge of human history. That is most obvious in the way we tell time, both as a culture and as a church. Whether you see time as "before the common era" and the "common era" or "before Christ" and "in the year of our Lord," still the turning point is the life, crucifixion, and resurrection of Jesus. The crucifixion not only shapes the way we as a church recount the date or year; it also serves to reconfigure our understanding of our own histories and mission. God is at work in human history, especially in this New Testament era, and his mission is to bring all things together in Jesus so that God might be all in all. Once again, we are brought back to God's glory and his determination to glorify himself.

The upshot of all this is that Edwards viewed history from a particular set of presuppositions. History serves to advance this particular purpose, namely, God's purpose in uniting all things in himself, his determination to glorify himself by emanating and remanating his own delight to and from his creation. This is not strictly "providential history" in the common understanding of the term; everything, after all, is providential because "God the great Creator of all things doth uphold, direct, dispose and govern all creatures, actions, and things, from the greatest even to the least, by his most wise and holy providence." Edwards's contribution is that cosmic redemption is the purpose in God's providential guidance; God's own glory is the end of all things. As Edwards put it, "All the great and mighty works of God from the fall of man to the end of the world, and reducible to this work [of redemption], and if seen in a right view of them, will appear as parts of it."[1]

Redemption, then, is at the center. That is what Edwards himself told the Princeton trustees in response to their invitation that he become the next president of the College of New Jersey. He wanted to produce a book from these sermons, one that would bring history and theology together in considering how each part "stands in reference to the great work of redemption by Jesus Christ; which I suppose is to be the grand design of all God's designs, and the *summum* and *ultimum* of all the divine dispensations and degrees; particularly considering all parts of the grand scheme in their historical order." God's purpose from

---

[1]Westminster Confession of Faith 5.1; Jonathan Edwards, "A History of the Work of Redemption," in *The Works of Jonathan Edwards* (hereafter *WJE*), vol. 9, *A History of the Work of Redemption*, ed. John F. Wilson (New Haven, CT: Yale University Press, 1989), 149.

eternity past was redemption; it is the sum and *telos* of the entire story and drives the continuing mission.[2]

Likewise, because redemption is at the center of God's eternal purpose, Jesus is at the center of Scripture. Edwards put it baldly: "Christ and his redemption are the great subject of the whole Bible." Wherever we look in Scripture, we expect to find something about Jesus and his work of redemption. "The whole book, both Old Testament and New, is filled up with gospel," Edwards averred, "with only this difference, that the Old Testament contains the gospel under a veil, but the New contains it unveiled, so that we may see the glory of the Lord with 'open face.'" Hence, God's people need to pay attention to the Old Testament. Far from being "out of date," it serves to "illustrate and confirm" the glorious doctrines of the New Testament. In fact, we will not understand fully the wonder of the gospel unless we see all of Scripture related to Jesus. His work and his person are the center because God's large purpose is to glorify himself by redeeming his world.[3]

Redemption Shadowed

From the fall of Adam until the coming of Jesus, the work of redemption was shadowed forth. And shadow is the right image: "The light that the church enjoyed from the fall of man till Christ came was like the light which we enjoy in the night, not the light of the sun directly but as reflected from the moon and stars, which light did foreshadow Christ to come." If Christ and his redemption are the sun, the center of God's story, then his shadows were cast backward into human history. God's people had some indication of what was to come through two means. One was the predictions that God gave through the prophets of the

---

[2] Jonathan Edwards to the trustees of the College of New Jersey, October 19, 1757, in *WJE*, vol. 16, *Letters and Personal Writings*, ed. George S. Claghorn (New Haven, CT: Yale University Press, 1998), 727–28. Surprisingly, very few have traced Edwards's redemptive-historical methodology; two who do are Stephen M. Clark, "Jonathan Edwards: The History of Redemption" (PhD diss., Drew University, 1986), and Avihu Zakai, *Jonathan Edwards's Philosophy of History: The Re-enchantment of the World in the Age of the Enlightenment* (Princeton, NJ: Princeton University Press, 2003).

[3] "A History of the Work of Redemption," *WJE*, 9:289–90.

Redeemer's coming. The other was through types that prefigured Christ's coming and work. Both served to point people to the coming redemption that would be found in the Messiah, the Redeemer of God's own people.[4]

Edwards's approach to Old Testament interpretation focused on typology. He held that there were three kinds of types in the Old Testament: institutional, providential, and personal. The sacrificial system was an example of an institutional type; the exodus was a providential type; and David was the great personal type of the Old Testament. This was because it was

> God's manner of old in the times of the Old Testament, from generation to generation, and even from the beginning of the world to the end of the Old Testament history, to represent divine things by outward signs, types and symbolical representations, and especially thus to typify and prefigure future events that he revealed by his Spirit and foretold by the prophets.

Each of these, and more beside, pointed forward to the work of redemption that Jesus would effect.[5]

First and Future Sacrifices

This redemptive work began right after the fall of Adam: Edwards claimed that "as soon as ever man fell Christ entered on his mediatorial work." The reason Adam was not destroyed immediately after the fall was that "Christ the eternal Son of God clothed himself with his mediatorial character and therein presented himself before the Father. He immediately stepped in between an holy, infinite, offended majesty and offending mankind, and was accepted in his interposition." And because Christ stepped forth as a mediator, Adam was shown mercy; without a mediator, there is no mercy for sinful humanity.[6]

---

[4]Ibid., 9:136.
[5]Ibid., 9:204; Jonathan Edwards, "Types of the Messiah," in *WJE*, vol. 11, *Typological Writings*, ed. Wallace E. Anderson and Mason I. Lowance Jr., with David Watters (New Haven, CT: Yale University Press, 1993), 202.
[6]"A History of the Work of Redemption," *WJE*, 9:129, 130.

For Adam, Christ's future sacrifice was declared in two ways. First, the promise of Genesis 3:15 declares that the coming seed of the woman would crush the head of the Enemy. Right at the beginning of human history, one of the great results of God's work of redemption was signaled: "God's design of subduing his enemies under the feet of his Son." And Christ's means of crushing and subduing his enemies would be through his death. This was the beginning of the work of redemption; from this point, God began to prepare for the coming of the woman's seed that would accomplish his redemptive purpose.[7]

Second, the custom of sacrifice began at this time to foreshadow the future sacrifice of Jesus. Edwards observed that "soon after this [promise] the custom of sacrificing was appointed to be a standing type of the sacrifice of Christ till he should come and offer up himself a sacrifice to God." In fact, it was probable that sacrifice was instituted immediately after the promise of Genesis 3:15 was given: "covenant and promise was the foundation on which the custom of sacrificing was built." And Christ's atoning sacrifice was pictured in the way that God shed the blood of animals that Adam and Eve's shame might be covered. Genesis 3:21 serves as "a lively figure of their being clothed with the righteousness of Christ." In particular, the entire scene "tended to establish in the minds of God's visible church the necessity of a propitiatory sacrifice in order to the deity's being atoned for sin." A Redeemer was coming to satisfy God's wrath and to cover sin.[8]

Enoch

The work of redemption not only shadows forth the death of Christ, but also pictures the resurrection of Christ and of his elect in him. That was part of the use to which Edwards put the biblical character Enoch from Genesis 5. In the midst of a litany of death, God's Word says that "Enoch walked with God, and he was not, for God took him" (Gen. 5:24). Edwards understood this "translation of Enoch" as "the first instance that ever was of

---

[7]Ibid., 9:134.
[8]Ibid., 9:134, 135, 136.

restoring the ruins of the fall with respect to the body." As such, it prefigured the larger truth that "all the bodies of the saints shall actually be redeemed: those that then shall have been dead, by a resurrection; and others that then be living, by causing them to pass under a glorious change." Such resurrection was intimately connected to the future resurrection of the Christ; even more, it taught the old covenant saints about the "future estate and of the future glorious reward of the saints in heaven."[9]

The Flood

The flood also served to shadow forth the coming redemption. As Noah and his family were saved by going through the floodwaters, they served to prefigure the salvation of the church. Connecting Genesis 6–9 to 1 Peter 3:20–21, Edwards argued:

> That water that washed away the filth of the world, that cleared the world of wicked men, was a type of the blood of Christ that takes away the sin of the world. That water that delivered Noah and his sons from their enemies is a type of that blood that delivers God's church from their sins, their worst enemies.

But the flood not only served as a sign of cleansing by Christ's blood; even after the emergence of Noah's family from the ark, there was sacrifice. In a world made "new," God promised not to destroy the earth, "signifying how, here too by the sacrifice of Christ, that God's favor is obtained and his people are in safety from God's destroying judgment and do obtain the blessing of the Lord." Christ's coming redemption once again is shadowed forth for God's people.[10]

Abraham

Abraham was a major figure in the history of the work of redemption. It was particularly during Abraham's time that "the covenant of grace was revealed and confirmed" more fully, as compared

---

[9]Ibid., 9:145–46.
[10]Ibid., 9:151, 152.

with previous generations. In particular, God gave Abraham five confirmations of his covenant of grace: Abraham's victory of Chedorlaomer in Genesis 14; the blessing of bread and wine brought by Melchizedek in the same chapter; the confirmation of God's promise by means of sacrifice in Genesis 15; the giving of the promised child in Genesis 18; and the deliverance of Isaac in Genesis 22. Each of these scenes served to point forward to Christ's future work: his victory over his enemies; the establishment of the Lord's Supper; the crucifixion; the coming of Jesus, the promised child; and the resurrection of Christ. The shadows would find their fulfillment in the coming Redeemer.[11]

The Exodus

Edwards also considered the exodus an important figure of the coming redemption. The exodus was "the most remarkable of all the Old Testament redemptions of God's church and that which was the greatest pledge and forerunner of the future redemption of Christ of any. . . . Indeed, it was the greatest type of Christ's redemption of any providential event whatsoever." And that was because at the heart of the exodus was the idea of redemption. Israel experienced "hard service and cruel bondage" under Pharaoh's rule far from the Promised Land. Moses was sent to redeem the church from its slavery, to lead it out of Egypt to the Promised Land. He did so through many "terrible judgments" upon the Egyptian enemies, but especially through the blood of the paschal lamb. In the same fashion, spiritually considered, human beings experience cruel bondage under Satan, a spiritual Pharaoh, as a result of their sin. Jesus was sent to redeem the church from their slavery and to lead them to heaven, the true Promised Land. He did so by triumphing over the principalities and powers through his miracles, but especially through his own bloody sacrifice. The exodus was the great type of Christ's great and eternal redemption.[12]

---

[11]Ibid., 9:165.
[12]Ibid., 9:175–76.

David

Another great type of Christ's work was David, the supreme king of Old Testament Israel. The Old Testament prophets as well as New Testament writers made repeated connections between David and the coming Messiah; Edwards noted Psalm 89:20; Isaiah 11:1; Jeremiah 23:5; 33:15; Ezekiel 34:23–24; 37:24; Luke 1:32; Acts 2:30; and Revelation 22:16 as examples. But the most important set of Davidic texts that point forward to Christ's work is 2 Samuel 7. There not only was God "solemnly preserving the covenant of grace with David," but he also promised "that the Messiah should be of his seed." The Messiah would establish David's throne forever; he would rule over the nations eternally. And this promise was at the heart of God's purpose in the everlasting covenant of grace: Isaiah 55:1–3 teaches that David's mercies would be offered by the Messiah to all who come to him. Redemption would come through David's greater son.[13]

Solomon

Edwards spent a great deal of time reflecting on how Solomon served as a type of Christ and his redemption. Solomon's very name means "peace"; when he was born, Nathan the prophet called him Jedidah, "beloved of the Lord"; he was promised the throne forever; and he was spoken of as God's son. All of these find their ultimate fulfillment in the Messiah. Other details fit in, such as the fact that Solomon's mother had once been the wife of a Hittite, "fitly denoting the honor that the prophecies represent that the Gentiles should have by their relation to the Messiah." Not only this, but also the promise that David, his father, made to Bathsheba that Solomon would certainly reign, representing "the sending of the Messiah and introducing the blessings of his reign was the grand promise and covenant and oath of God to his church of old, to Abraham, Isaac and Jacob, and in David's and the prophet's times." Above all, "the peaceful, happy and

---

[13]Ibid., 9:204–5; 214.

glorious reign of Solomon" parallels the future "introduction of the glorious day of the Messiah's reign."[14]

Tribe of Judah

The rest of the Old Testament story focuses on how God preserved his people, despite their corruptions and their eventual exile, so that the Messiah might come. Edwards particularly noted how the tribe of Judah was "remarkably preserved." Several times in the Old Testament, Judah was "upon the brink of ruin and just ready to be swallowed up," but God delivered them from Shishak, king of Egypt, during Rehoboam's reign, from the Moabites and Ammonites during Jehoshaphat's reign, and from the Assyrians during Hezekiah's reign. And even during the Babylonian exile, God was preparing the ground for the redemption by means of Christ's crucifixion: curing God's people of their "itch after idolatry"; taking away their king and diminishing the glory of their temple; and permitting the loss of the temple artifacts. Edwards declared, "Thus the lights of the Old Testament go out on the approach of the glorious sun of righteousness."[15]

Redemption Fulfilled

The shadows of the coming redemption were deepened and renewed as the centuries drew closer to the "fullness of time" (Gal. 4:4). Those shadows found their fulfillment in Jesus of Nazareth. Even before he unpacked how Jesus brought about redemption, Edwards observed that the Old Testament

> strongly argues that Jesus of Nazareth is indeed the Son of God, and the savior of the world, and so that the Christian religion is the true religion, seeing that Christ is the very person so evidentially pointed at in all the great dispensations of God's providence from the very fall of man, and was so undoubtedly in such a multitude of instances foretold from age to age, and shadowed forth in a vast variety of types and figures.

[14]"Types of the Messiah," *WJE*, 11:276, 277, 279, 281.
[15]"A History of the Work of Redemption," *WJE*, 9:234–37, 251, 254.

Jesus was the great antitype of all the Old Testament types; he was the promised Redeemer of God's elect; and he was the sun of righteousness that cast the shadows back into the old covenant.[16]

Moral Government Theory?

But what exactly did Jesus accomplish on the cross?[17] At least one historian has suggested that Edwards may have held a view of the atonement known as the "moral governmental theory." The moral governmental theory suggests that God as the great moral governor of the universe had to punish humankind for sin in order for his government to be just. In his mercy, God sent Jesus to die as a punishment for sin, to demonstrate that sin deserves death, and to make it safe for him to justify those who repent and believe in him. Jesus was not actually a "substitute" who suffered the punishment for a specific people; rather, his death was of such value that it could save every human should each one repent and believe.[18]

Did Edwards actually hold to such a position? When one examines the position he stakes out in the sermons that make up "A History of the Work of Redemption," it is clear he did not. Rather, Edwards taught that Jesus died as a substitutionary atonement, bearing God's wrath on behalf of the elect. There were three key words in Edwards's discussion of Jesus's work of redemption: *purchase, satisfaction,* and *humiliation.*

Christ's Purchase of Our Redemption

First, Edwards argues that Christ *purchased* redemption for the elect. Upon completion of Christ's redemptive suffering, "the utmost farthing was paid of the price of the salvation of every

[16]Ibid., 9:281.
[17]It is a bit surprising how few studies there are on Edwards's view of atonement, especially in the light of the directions his students went on the topic. For one of the few, see Michael Jinkins, *A Comparative Study in the Theology of Atonement in Jonathan Edwards and John McLeod Campbell: Atonement and the Character of God* (San Francisco: Mellen Research University Press, 1993).
[18]See Allen C. Guelzo, *Edwards on the Will: A Century of American Theological Debate* (Middletown, CT: Wesleyan University Press, 1989), 132–35.

one of the elect." Nothing about the Old Testament sacrifices enabled them to purchase redemption. "But as soon as Christ was incarnate, then the purchase began immediately without any delay." Every aspect of Christ's life on earth "was taken up in this purchase." With the death, burial, and resurrection of Jesus, "the purchase was entirely and completely finished"; nothing more could or would be done after Jesus's resurrection. What Jesus came to do was "to purchase a never-ending life for man."[19]

Christ's Satisfaction of Our Debt

What did Edwards mean when he talked about "purchase"? He defined the word in terms of *satisfaction*.

> I would show what is here intended by Christ's purchasing of redemption. And there are two things that are intended by it, viz. his satisfaction and merit. All is done by the price that Christ lays down. But the price that Christ laid down does two things: it pays our debt and so it satisfies by its intrinsic value and agreement between the Father and Son; it procures a title for us to happiness and so it merits.

And so, when Jesus purchased redemption for his people, he did so by paying or satisfying our debt. Indeed, "the satisfaction of Christ consists in his answering those demands that the law laid on man that were consequent on the breach of the law, which was suffering the penalty of the law." The covenant of works must be fulfilled; it has been broken from Adam's time to the present day, and judgment has been the result. Jesus came to satisfy the wrath of God for the sin of the elect, on the basis of which humans come to God through Christ, pleading the satisfaction that Christ already made on the cross.[20]

Indeed, this satisfaction happened as Christ's death was imputed to the elect who are united to Jesus by faith. Jesus "was

---

[19]"A History of the Work of Redemption," *WJE*, 9:295, 305.
[20]Ibid., 9:304, 305. See also, Jonathan Edwards, "The 'Miscellanies,' no. 245," in *WJE*, vol. 13, *The "Miscellanies," a–500*, ed. Thomas A. Schafer (New Haven, CT: Yale University Press, 1994), 359–60.

willing to take their sins to himself and have them put on his account, and to bear the punishment himself." This happened as God looked upon Jesus and the elect as one and the same. Jesus "took them into a union with himself; so that they may be called members of him, may be called his body, may be called his wife: so that if the husband pays her debt, the wife may go free; if the head suffers, the members and body go free." This union with Christ means that Christ was "willing to stand in their stead in misery and torment" so that the elect could go free. In the same way that "Adam's sin is their sin" so by virtue of "the union of their persons with Christ's person," his death is theirs. "They are made so much one that his death belongs to them; they own it, it is their death." Such a union was ultimately forged by love.

> If Christ so loves men that when they are to be destroyed, he out of mere love is willing to take their destruction upon himself, or what is equivalent to their destruction so that they may be saved; then he loves them so, that he may be looked upon as being the same; for this reason, because then his love is such, that of itself it puts him thoroughly in the beloved's stead, even to the utmost, in the most extreme case. Such love as this makes a thorough union.

God looks at sinners united to Christ by his dying love, receives his death as their own, and sets them free.[21]

Christ could offer such a satisfaction because of his divine nature. The sin of human beings is infinitely heinous and deserves the full, eternal wrath of an infinitely holy God. But, Edwards said:

> as the infinite dignity of Christ's person answered the eternity of punishment, so his dying with a sense of this his dignity, and the infinite happiness he had before the world was, answered the sense of the eternity of the punishment in the damned. He had for the present lost infinitely more than the damned lose, because his blessedness in the love and communion with God was infinitely greater.

---

[21] "The 'Miscellanies,' no. b," *WJE*, 13:165; "The 'Miscellanies,' no. 281," *WJE*, 13:380.

In fact, the eternal death promised in the threat to Adam in Genesis 2:17 was borne in full by Christ.[22]

Christ's Humiliation

Christ offered satisfaction for the wrath of God primarily by his *humiliation*. Everything connected to Christ's incarnation was "propitiatory or satisfactory." Edwards observed that "not only proper suffering, but all abasement and depression of the state or circumstance of mankind below its primitive honor and dignity, such as his body's remaining under death, and body and soul remaining separate, and other things that might be mentioned, are the judicial fruits of sin." Christ's humiliation extended to the fact that the Lawgiver had to obey the laws that he created for his subjects, and in so doing Christ fulfilled the covenant of works that had been broken by Adam and left unfulfilled. It also extended to his temptation in the wilderness, where he was tested by one of his own creation. Edwards notes that "[Christ] got the victory. He who had such success with the first Adam had none with the second." At each point of his humiliation, Jesus fulfilled the law's demands for perfect obedience. What the first Adam failed to do, the second Adam did.[23]

However, the greatest and most glorious example of Christ's redemptive humiliation was his death upon the cross. In his dying on the cross, Jesus "made satisfaction to the justice of God for the sins of men." All that the law threatened, all that was required to satisfy divine justice, everything that vindictive justice demanded, all the debt of the elect—all was paid, all was done. This was the great work toward which all human history pointed and from which the rest of human history would flow. Nothing more was needed; nothing more could be added.[24]

---

[22]"The 'Miscellanies,' no. 319," *WJE*, 13:401; "The 'Miscellanies,' no. 265," *WJE*, 13:371; "The 'Miscellanies,' no. 357," *WJE*, 13:429. Edwards summarized much of this in a single entry in his "Miscellanies": see Jonathan Edwards, "The 'Miscellanies,' no. 779," in *WJE*, vol. 18, *The "Miscellanies," 501–832*, ed. Ava Chamberlain (New Haven, CT: Yale University Press, 2000), 434–49.
[23]"A History of the Work of Redemption," *WJE*, 9:306, 305, 309, 315.
[24]Ibid., 9:318, 327, 331, 342.

Christ's redemptive death not only accomplished the salvation of the elect. It also laid the foundation for the fulfillment of the promise of Genesis 3:15: "the overthrow of Satan's kingdom" and the subjection of all things to the triune God. How would God accomplish his glory in working out this redemptive purpose? How would God make all things new?

CHAPTER 4

The *Summum* and *Ultimum*

Consummation

God's mission was to unite all things in himself, things on earth, above earth, under the earth. Only in this way would he be glorified; only in this way would the love and delight that characterized the triune God before time began grow and flourish. But the means by which God would unite all things in himself was redemption: through Jesus, God was redeeming a people for himself so that they might reflect his glory back to him and grow to enjoy him forever.

Edwards signaled this larger, more cosmic vision of God's purpose in the way he talked about the work of redemption. As noted earlier, he told the College of New Jersey trustees that he supposed that "the great work of redemption by Jesus Christ" was "the grand design of all God's designs, and the *summum* and *ultimum* of all the divine dispensations and degrees." The language of "ultimate" and "highest" purpose immediately takes one to Edwards's understanding of the end for which God created the world. After a discussion that distinguishes "chief" end from "ultimate" end, he wrote, "It appears reasonable to suppose that it was what God had respect to as an ultimate end of his creating the world, to communicate his own infinite fullness of good." Yet, how can God communicate his own infinite goodness to those who are sinners, rebels, and deserters? He seeks and saves the lost through the Redeemer, Jesus.[1]

And so, redemption stands as the central means by which God accomplishes his larger purpose of communicating his own infinite fullness of good to his creation. As Edwards put it in his sermon series "A History of the Work of Redemption":

> From what has been said we may argue that the Work of Redemption is the greatest of all God's works that we have any notice of, and that 'tis the end of all his other works. It appears plainly from what has been said, that this work is the principal of all God's works of providence, and that all other works of providence are reducible hither; they are all subordinate to the great affair of redemption. We see that all revolutions in the world are to subserve to this grand design, so that the Work of Redemption is, as it were, the sum of God's works of providence.

The end, design, or purpose finds its ultimate summing up in redemption.[2]

But this redemption that God is bringing to his world is not simply the redeeming of individual souls. As historian Harry Stout has put it, Edwards has a "tri-world" vision when it comes to understanding God's work: heaven and hell as well as earth are involved in this cosmic redemptive work that God is doing. At

---

[1] Jonathan Edwards to the trustees of the College of New Jersey, October 19, 1757, in *The Works of Jonathan Edwards* (hereafter *WJE*), vol. 16, *Letters and Personal Writings*, ed. George S. Claghorn (New Haven, CT: Yale University Press, 1998), 727–28; Jonathan Edwards, "The End for Which God Created the World," in *WJE*, vol. 8, *Ethical Writings*, ed. Paul Ramsay (New Haven, CT: Yale University Press, 1989), 433.

[2] Jonathan Edwards, "A History of the Work of Redemption," in *WJE*, vol. 9, *A History of the Work of Redemption*, ed. John F. Wilson (New Haven, CT: Yale University Press, 1989), 512–13.

the end of human history, there will be a new heaven and new earth, but earth will be drawn up into heaven as the place of eternal rest. Edwards thought it both biblical and rational that

> the settled and everlasting abode of the righteous after the resurrection, shall not be here upon this earth, but in heaven, in that world of glory where the man Christ Jesus now is. . . . 'Tis fit that in the consummation of all things, that all things should be gathered together to God, that the less should remove and be brought home to the greater, and not the greater change place to come to the less.

God is drawing all things into himself, uniting them in himself in heavenly splendor, delight, and glory.[3]

God's mission in human history, then, is to advance this cause of gathering together all things and causing all things to partake of his glory. The means is the advancing work of redemption that was shadowed in the old covenant and fulfilled in the coming of Jesus, the Redeemer of God's elect. Between the first and second comings of Christ, the work of redemption continues to advance in real-time history through the work of the Spirit of Jesus. And the Spirit works through cyclical outpourings of himself, bringing reformation and revival.

Revival History

Edwards viewed history from the cross of Jesus to the end of human history in four broad movements: the work of the apostles; the destruction of "the heathen Roman empire" by Emperor Constantine; the destruction of the Antichrist; and the coming of Christ in judgment. Within those four broad movements, there are ebbs and flows, times when the church is more successful and times when it is nearly defunct. And yet, God maintains a

[3]Harry S. Stout, "Jonathan Edwards's Tri-World Vision," in *The Legacy of Jonathan Edwards: American Religion and the Evangelical Tradition*, ed. D. G. Hart, Sean Michael Lucas, and Stephen J. Nichols (Grand Rapids: Baker, 2003), 27–46; Jonathan Edwards, "The 'Miscellanies,' no. 634," in *WJE*, vol. 18, *The "Miscellanies," no. 501–832*, ed. Ava Chamberlain (New Haven, CT: Yale University Press, 2000), 161.

redeemed people for his own glory and restores the church to influence and importance.[4]

The way God maintains his people is through the regular outpouring of the Holy Spirit. Human history is driven forward through reformation and revival. Early in his sermons on "A History of the Work of Redemption," Edwards noted that

> from the fall of man to this day wherein we live the Work of Redemption in its effect has mainly been carried on by remarkable pourings out of the Spirit of God. Though there be a more constant influence of God's Spirit always in some degree attending his ordinances, yet the way in which the greatest things have been done towards carrying on this work always has been by remarkable pourings out of the Spirit at special seasons of mercy.[5]

And that is how God worked in the Old Testament; he preserved his church through revival. "And [God] was pleased several times after exceeding great degeneracy, and things seemed to come to extremity, and religion seemed to be come to its last gasp," Edwards declared, "then God granted blessed revivals by remarkable outpourings of his Spirit, particularly in Hezekiah's and Josiah's times." Times of covenantal renewal in the Old Testament period served as means of the outpouring of God's Spirit. Deuteronomy 29 serves as one example during which "we find that such solemn renovations of the covenant commonly accompanied any remarkable pouring out of the Spirit, causing a general reformation."[6]

However, it is particularly in this New Testament era, after the resurrection and ascension of Jesus, that history moves forward through the outpouring of God's Spirit and revival. And so, in Edwards's telling, the church endures opposition from without—persecution from the Jews, the Romans, the Roman Catholic Church, and the final Antichrist. And she knows decay

---

[4]"A History of the Work of Redemption," *WJE*, 9:351.
[5]Ibid., 9:141.
[6]Ibid., 9:233, 192.

from within—heresy, luxury, ignorance, and folly. Indeed, the main story line in the history of God's work of redemption is affliction and persecution for the church, "excepting where the day is, as it were, shorted by some intermissions and times of respite, which God gives for the elect's sake."[7]

One of the particular days of respite was the Reformation. During that time, "God began gloriously to revive his church again and advance the kingdom of his Son after such a dismal night of darkness as had been before from the rise of Antichrist to that time." While God was reviving his church through Luther, Zwingli, and Calvin, the Enemy of God was using all his power to oppose him—councils, open war, persecution, political plotting were all means that Satan used to try to stop this time of revival and renewal. Failing that, the Enemy began to use "corrupt opinions": Anabaptists, Quakers, Socinians, Arminians, deists. It appeared that the church might be overwhelmed.[8]

A Surprising Work of God

But in Edwards's own day, "a surprising work of God" happened. What some would later call "a great awakening" occurred throughout Anglo-America, transforming lives, churches, and communities. As a result, there was a reformation of doctrine and a renewed desire to reach nations and people groups with the gospel. But there was also tremendous controversy, as people tried to understand what God was doing, and some used by the Enemy sought to oppose, persecute, and shut down the revival.[9]

Many contemporary Christians are aware that Edwards reflected deeply on the meaning of the Great Awakening, especially in the light of God's larger, cosmic purposes of redemption and self-glorification. Like many intellectuals of his day, Edwards believed that human history advanced from east to west: from

---

[7] Ibid., 9:409.
[8] Ibid., 9:422, 431.
[9] Ibid., 9:436. I understand the period known as "the Great Awakening" to extend from the 1734–1735 revival in Northampton through 1742. For more on the period, see particularly Frank Lambert, *Inventing the "Great Awakening"* (Princeton, NJ: Princeton University Press, 1999).

the ancient peoples that dominated the Bible and stretched from Egypt to China, through Europe and then to the Americas. And so, the coming of the gospel to the Americas was pregnant with redemptive-historical meaning.

> I think we may well look upon the discovery of so great a part of the world as America and bringing the gospel into it, as one thing by which divine providence is preparing the way for the future glorious times of the church when Satan's kingdom shall be overthrown not only throughout the Roman empire but throughout the whole habitable globe, on every side and in all its continents.[10]

Because of this intellectual commitment, Edwards viewed the Great Awakening in larger, cosmic terms. "'Tis not unlikely that this work of God's Spirit, that is so extraordinary and wonderful, is the dawning, or at least a prelude, of that glorious work of God, so often foretold in Scripture, which in the progress and issue of it, shall renew the world of mankind," Edwards claimed. "And there are many things that make it probably that this work will begin in America." After all, the Americas are a remote part of the world, and the gospel has progressed from Asia to Europe and now to America. Once the gospel covers the world as the waters cover the seas, would not that be the ushering in of the millennial age?[11]

In addition, the pouring out of God's Spirit in eighteenth-century New England motivated a new surge in missionary activity and prayer. Men like David Brainerd were part of a new breed of missionaries. Converted or renewed during the Great Awakening, they were determined to bring the gospel to Native Americans who had been under the control of the Devil from their earliest days. Indeed, Edwards believed that at the Tower of Babel "the devil afterwards led many nations unto remote parts of the world

[10] "A History of the Work of Redemption," *WJE*, 9:435.
[11] Jonathan Edwards, "Some Thoughts Concerning the Present Revival of Religion (1742)," in *WJE*, vol. 4, *The Great Awakening*, ed. C. C. Goen (New Haven, CT: Yale University Press, 1972), 353.

to that end to get 'em out of the way of the gospel, led 'em into America." But Edwards's disciples like Brainerd, Gideon Hawley, Eleazar Wheelock, and his son, Jonathan Edwards Jr., all sought to bring the gospel to the Native Americans in an attempt to advance the work of God's Spirit in these last days.[12]

Worldwide prayer for the continued outpouring of God's Spirit and advancement of international missions also was part of the Great Awakening inheritance. Though the Great Awakening was another day of God's renewal, reformation, and revival, "there is *yet remaining* a great advancement of the interest of religion and the kingdom of Christ in this world, by an abundant outpouring of the Spirit of God, far greater and more extensive than ever yet has been." Until that day, God's people should unite in prayer for such a great, final outpouring of God's Spirit because prayer is "the principal means that the Spirit of God makes us of to carry on his work of grace."[13]

Read in these terms, Edwards viewed the Great Awakening as part of the final defeat and destruction of the Antichrist. It was not the last great revival before the millennial period, but it was another foretaste of what was coming. Not only was it a means to prevent his church from being ruined, but revivals like the Great Awakening were the means that God would use to drive history forward to the new heavens and new earth and the drawing up of all things into God himself.

Kingdom Come

If the Great Awakening was not the final outpouring of God's Spirit, what did the future hold for God's church and world? Edwards was committed to an understanding of world history that saw the ages divided into more or less seven one-thousand-

---

[12]"A History of the Work of Redemption," *WJE*, 9:155. For more on New England missions and Edwards's redemptive vision for it, see Gerald R. McDermott, *Jonathan Edwards Confronts the Gods: Christian Theology, Enlightenment Religion, and Non-Christian Faiths* (New York: Oxford University Press, 2000), 194–206, and Stephen J. Nichols, "The Last of the Mohican Missionaries: Jonathan Edwards at Stockbridge," in *The Legacy of Jonathan Edwards*, 47–63.
[13]Jonathan Edwards, "An Humble Attempt," in *WJE*, vol. 5, *Apocalyptic Writings*, ed. Stephen J. Stein (New Haven, CT: Yale University Press, 1977), 329, 322.

year blocks. He related these ages to the days of creation: "The first 6000 years are 6 days of labor, and the seventh is a Sabbath rest." That seventh thousand-year "day" is the millennium, which is not the end of human history but rather a foretaste of the new heavens and new earth. If one agreed with scholarship from the period that biblical creation was around 4000 BC, then six thousand years would mean that the millennium would begin in AD 2000. Not coincidentally, that would be the year that Satan's kingdom would "receive its finishing stroke."[14]

And so, what did Edwards foresee between his day and the coming millennium? And what would the millennium itself bring? Before the millennium, there would be dark days for the church. The Antichrist would set itself up in the church, "pretending to be vested with the power of God himself, as head of the church." Edwards identified this with the Roman Catholic Church, and in this he was not alone; the Westminster Confession of Faith as originally written in 1647 did the same. There would also be a renewal of suffering, persecution, and even martyrdom. In fact, "it will be a very dark time with respect to the interests of religion in the world"; there will be "little religion" worldwide in those days.[15]

At that time, "[God's] Spirit shall be gloriously poured out for the wonderful revival and propagation of religion." While the Scripture does not make clear where this pouring out of the Spirit will begin, yet the Spirit will bring men who are mighty in preaching God's Word, filled "with knowledge and wisdom and a fervent zeal for the promoting the kingdom of Christ and the salvation of souls and propagating the gospel in the world." The net result of this powerful preaching will be a "reviving of those holy doctrines of religion that are now chiefly ridiculed in the world." Heresy will be overthrown, and the Roman Catholic Church undone. Conversions will increase as multitudes "from many nations" believe the gospel.[16]

---

[14]Jonathan Edwards, "Apocalypse Series, no. 16," in *WJE*, 5:129. See also "An Humble Attempt," *WJE*, 5:394.

[15]"A History of the Work of Redemption," *WJE*, 9:451, 457; Westminster Confession of Faith 25.6.

[16]"A History of the Work of Redemption," *WJE*, 9:460, 461.

Certainly, there will be demonic opposition. The last great opposition of God's purposes will come. "All the forces of Antichrist, and also Mohammedanism and heathenism, should be united, all the forces of Satan's visible kingdom through the whole world of mankind." This great "battle," a mighty conflict or struggle between the united forces of the Roman Catholic Church, Islam, and paganism against the true, biblical (Protestant) church, will ultimately lead to a rout of God's enemies and final defeat of Satan himself.[17]

And the fall of Satan's empire will usher in the millennium, a period of great bliss and advancement of God's reign. The good news of the gospel will run far and wide. "The word of God shall have a speedy and swift progress through the earth." The Jewish people, in particular, will experience conversion so that "all Israel will be saved" (Rom. 11:26). The nations that were formerly without the gospel will be enlightened. And the result will be that "the kingdom of Christ shall in the most strict and literal sense extend to all nations and the whole earth."[18]

As God's Word advances, "all shall agree in the sure, great and important doctrines of the gospel"; there will be no more heresies to divide and distract the church. This age will be "a time of great light and knowledge" where formerly ignorant nations shall produce great works. "It may be hoped that then many of the Negroes and Indians will be divines, and that excellent books will be published in Africa, in Ethiopia, in Turkey." As the nations contribute to biblical and doctrinal knowledge, "there shall then be a wonderful unraveling [of] the difficulties in the doctrines of religion, and clearing up [of] seeming inconsistencies." It will be like "heaven on earth."[19]

Most importantly, the gospel will have such an effect that "holiness shall become general." While there may be some who remain unconverted, still sin, evil, and unrighteousness will be suppressed. Religion will have the upper hand in the world, and

[17]Ibid., 9:463–64.
[18]Ibid., 9:466, 467, 469–70, 473.
[19]Ibid., 9:467, 480–81.

even the "great men of the world" will "devote all to Christ and his church." There will be no more wars in the world or in the church. Rather, peace and love will reign between rulers and ruled, ministers and people, fathers and children. And the result will be that "all the world [shall] be united in peace and love in one amiable society; all nations, in all parts, on every side of the globe, shall then be knit together in sweet harmony, all parts of God's church assisting and promoting the knowledge and spiritual good one of another." It will be a blissful time, in Edwards's view.[20]

Eschaton

And yet, the millennium is not the *eschaton*, the end of time. While millennial bliss will last a long time, the history of the work of redemption has one last moment of opposition before it is consummated. In Edwards's thinking, there will be final, great apostasy. Satan will be released once again to wreck havoc on the church. After extending to the ends of the earth, the church will again "be reduced to narrow limits." Having broken free from the restraint of the church, people will again "abuse their prosperity to serve their lust and corruption." It appears for a time that the church itself might be overthrown by the "most aggravated wickedness that ever it was."[21]

But Christ in his mercy will intervene. "Christ will appear in the glory of his father with all the holy angels coming on the clouds of heaven," Edwards held. Importantly, it is in his role as Redeemer that Jesus will appear. "He through whom this redemption has all along been carried on, he shall appear in the sight of the world, the light of his glory shall break forth." For the wicked, the sight will be stunning. They will be filled with wailing, shrieking, horror, terror, and amazement. But for the righteous, "it shall be a most joyful and glorious sight to them." And that is because the work of redemption is done: "The whole

[20]Ibid., 9:483–84.
[21]Ibid., 9:488, 489.

church shall be completely and eternally freed from all persecution and molestation from wicked men and devils."[22]

The wicked will be judged, but the righteous will receive their reward: they will experience the resurrection with their bodies and souls reunited; the whole church shall be gathered together; and "the whole church shall be perfectly and forever delivered from this present evil world, forever forsake this cursed ground." They will enter into the new heavens where Christ has his throne, never to return to earth. The wicked will remain on the earth to be consumed by God's fiery wrath. The earth will become like a large furnace and sinners will be tormented forever here.[23]

And what will that heaven be like? It will be a world of love because "the Spirit shall be poured forth in perfect love into every heart." Not only this, but God himself dwells there as the cause and fountain of love. Because God himself is love and because God is an all-sufficient being, "he is a full and overflowing and inexhaustible fountain of love." God communicates love among himself.

> The infinite essential love of God is, as it were, an infinite and eternal mutual holy energy between the Father and the Son, a pure, holy act whereby the Deity becomes nothing but an infinite and unchangeable act of love, which proceeds from both the Father and the Son. Thus divine love has its seat in the Deity as it is exercised within the Deity, or in God toward himself.

And as God loves himself, he delights to communicate his love to his people and to receive back again his love from them.[24]

Heaven will be a place of excellency. Once again, that is because God himself is the most excellent of beings. There will be none but perfectly lovely objects there; the music will be perfectly lovely; the air and water will be perfectly pure. "There shall be no string out of tune to cause any jar in the harmony of that world,

---

[22]Ibid., 9:494, 495, 496.
[23]Ibid., 9:496, 345, 505.
[24]Jonathan Edwards, "Charity and Its Fruits," in *WJE*, 8:367, 373. Edwards wrote of these things more briefly in "A History of the Work of Redemption," *WJE*, 9:506–10.

no unpleasant note to cause any discord," Edwards wrote. And there will be harmony between all the residents of that place. "All that whole society rejoice in each other's happiness; for the love of benevolence is perfect in them." Further,

> The love of benevolence is delighted in beholding the prosperity of another, as the love of complacence is delighted in viewing the beauty of another. So that the superior prosperity of those who are higher in glory is so far from being any damp to the happiness of saints of lower degree that it is an addition to it, or a part of it.

There will be a "sweet and perfect harmony" in that heavenly society because love reigns.[25]

The love for God and one another that the saints experience will be wholly satisfying. Love will be mutual in the new heavens. "As the saints will love God with an inconceivable ardor of heart, and to the utmost of their capacity; so they will know that he has loved them from eternity, and that he still loves them and will love them to eternity." Not only this, but the saints' love for one another will be "mutual and answerable" as well; none will be unloved in heaven. Moreover, there will be nothing to clog the exercise of our love. There will be freedom in expression and freedom from fear and embarrassment as we love each other. And yet, this love will be expressed with "perfect decency and wisdom." All the saints shall be "one society, yea, one family."[26]

And heaven itself will be a garden of pleasures. Edwards put it memorably: "Heaven itself, the place of habitation, is a garden of pleasures, a heavenly paradise fitted in all respects for an abode of heavenly lovers, a place where they may have sweet society and perfect enjoyment of each other's love." No more sorrow, no more fear, no more shame: only holy pleasure and heavenly love.[27]

The end for which God created the world will be accomplished. Redemption will secure the emanation and remanation

---

[25] "Charity and Its Fruits," *WJE*, 8:371, 375, 376.
[26] Ibid., 8:377, 378, 379, 380.
[27] Ibid., 8:382.

of God's love, the drawing up of God's people into the very love that God has for himself, the enjoyment forever of God's own glory. And it will be excellent.

> Every saint there is a note in a concert of music which sweetly harmonizes with every other note, and all together employed wholly in praising God and the Lamb; and so all helping one another to their utmost to express their love of the whole society to the glorious Father and Head of it, and to pour back love into the fountain of love, whence they are supplied and filled with love and with glory.[28]

---

[28]Ibid., 8:386.

73

Part Two

REDEMPTION APPLIED

CHAPTER 5

A Divine and Supernatural Light

When Jonathan Edwards first preached his sermon "A Divine and Supernatural Light" to his congregation in August 1733, he was twenty-nine years old. For most of his life, he had been fascinated by light, both natural and supernatural. He had spent a great deal of time thinking about and working on "optics," a branch of "natural philosophy" (as science was then called) that focused specifically on light. For example, around 1723, when Edwards was doing graduate study at Yale, he wrote essays on the rainbow and light rays. These were largely mathematical exercises, but they also highlighted the importance of proportion and consent, terms so important to Edwards's understanding of beauty.[1]

However, it was particularly as an image of something supernatural that Edwards used "light" to such great effect. In one

---

[1]Both of these essays are found in *The Works of Jonathan Edwards* (hereafter *WJE*), vol. 6, *Scientific and Philosophical Writings*, ed. Wallace E. Anderson (New Haven, CT: Yale University Press, 1980), 296–304.

reflection, writing in his collection on "Images of Divine Things," Edwards observed that "the beautiful variety of the colors of light was designed as a type of the various beauties and graces of the Spirit of God." Particularly, "the colors of the rainbow" are used in Scripture to display the variegated glory and beauty of God. Colors and light display the moral goodness of God, but they also display the virtues and graces that appear in the saints through the work of the Spirit. The Spirit of God, like white light, contains all the manifold moral beauty and glory of God himself; he delights to display this in the lives of his people.[2]

Perhaps his earliest sermonic use of the light metaphor was in a sermon preached sometime in 1722 or 1723, around the time he was writing his essays on the rainbow and light rays. In this sermon, drawing from John 8:12, Edwards held that Christ is "the light of the world." On the surface, this seems to be a repetition of the biblical text, but what makes the sermon noteworthy is the use to which light is put. Light is viewed as "a most excellent and glorious similitude" because God the Father is "an infinite fountain of light," which Jesus as God's Son communicates. In fact, Jesus is the light of the world in the same fashion as the sun. As the sun shines on the entire earth and lights it, so Jesus shines on the world, universally offering his light as the sun of righteousness. As light, he shines in the darkness, makes all things manifest, displays his beauty and glory, quickens and revives those in darkness, and causes all spiritual fruit to grow in the lives of those who trust in him.[3]

A more extended meditation on light, one that would parallel his later development in "A Divine and Supernatural Light," was

---

[2]Jonathan Edwards, "Images of Divine Things," in *WJE*, vol. 11, *Typological Writings*, ed. Wallace E. Anderson, Mason I. Lowance Jr., with David Watters (New Haven, CT: Yale University Press, 1993), 67–69. Edwards also reflected upon the rainbow in his "Miscellanies": see Jonathan Edwards, "The 'Miscellanies,' nos. 362 and 370," in *WJE*, vol. 13, *The "Miscellanies," a–500*, ed. Thomas A. Schafer (New Haven, CT: Yale University Press, 1994), 434, 442, and Jonathan Edwards, "Notes on Scripture, no. 348," in *WJE*, vol. 15, *Notes on Scripture*, ed. Stephen J. Stein (New Haven, CT: Yale University Press, 1998), 329–35.
[3]Jonathan Edwards, "Christ, the Light of the World," in *WJE*, vol. 10, *Sermons and Discourses, 1720–1723*, ed. Wilson H. Kimnach (New Haven, CT: Yale University Press, 1992), 533–50.

his 1723 sermon "A Spiritual Understanding of Divine Things Denied to the Unregenerate." Reflecting on 1 Corinthians 2:14, Edwards drew a distinction between the knowledge that natural men have and that which spiritual men have. Natural men possess "notional knowledge," or understanding that consists simply in "notions." This knowledge may be large, orthodox, and even somewhat influential, but it is not knowledge that leads to conversion and hence is not "spiritual knowledge."[4]

Spiritual men, on the other hand, have spiritual knowledge. "This spiritual knowledge of divine things consists in a certain clear apprehension and a lively infixed sensibleness of them." Here Edwards introduced two key words involving his theory of knowledge: *apprehension* and *sense/sensation/sensibleness*. Spiritual knowledge is not just apprehension; rather, there is a sensibility that affects the individual—it is a "lively apprehension." One metaphor of this kind of spiritual knowledge is light: "This spiritual understanding is like a gleam of light that breaks in upon the soul through a gloomy darkness. Of all the similitudes that are made use of in Scripture to describe to us this spiritual understanding, light is that which doth most fully represent it and is oftenest used."[5]

In this sermon, Edwards divided spiritual light in three ways: "First, 'tis a sight of the truth and reality of spiritual things; second, of the excellency of divine and spiritual things; third, an experimental understanding of the operation of God's Spirit." As he unpacked these three sets of ideas, he was particularly interested in stressing that a spiritual sight of Christ's light causes the individual to "feel," to be affected by the excellency of spiritual truth; this in turn makes spiritual truth *real*. Unbelievers know nothing about spiritual truth except by "hearsay"; it is merely "notional" to them. But to believers, "God has given a glance, opened to the immediate view of their minds, and there breaks

[4]Jonathan Edwards, "A Spiritual Understanding of Divine Things Denied to the Unregenerate," in *WJE*, vol. 14, *Sermons and Discourses, 1723–1729*, ed. Kenneth P. Minkema (New Haven, CT: Yale University Press, 1997), 72–74.
[5]Ibid., 14:75–77.

in upon their souls such a heavenly sweetness, such a sense of the amiableness, as wonderfully affects the heart, and even transforms it." Spiritual knowledge/light makes us new human beings.[6]

A third reflection is helpful along this line. In his "Miscellanies," a private notebook of theological thought, Edwards connected the image of light to God's own being as triune. "God is said to be light and love. Light is his understanding or idea, which is his Son; love is the Holy Spirit. We are expressly told that Christ is the light." Here is a parallel to Edwards's other Trinitarian speculation. Earlier, following the psychological analogy, he said that God is God, the idea of God, and the delight that God takes in his own idea. Now, he says that God is light, the Son is the reflection of light, and the Spirit is the love the light has for his own self. And when divine light is communicated to the soul, what could it be other than God's own being?[7]

It would not be surprising to realize that for Edwards, heaven is not only a world of love, but also a world of light. And the light of that world will be Christ's own light flowing from himself to and through others. "The light of the heavenly regions shall be the brightness of glorified bodies, and especially their countenances, but chiefly of the man Christ Jesus, and the glory of God." The bodies and faces of the saints "shall be some way or other a communication of the light of Christ; and then the difference will be rather in degree of brightness than kind." On the earth humans delight in the light of the sun; it is "sweet and the sensation is pleasant to the mind." But if God is light and the world of heaven is light, "how delightful a place then is heaven, with its [light] so much more fine, more harmonious, more bright, but yet easy and pleasant to behold!"[8]

Each of these reflections and sermons bears striking resemblances to Edwards's best and most mature statement of how God's light enters the soul. In part, when Edwards preached "A Divine and Supernatural Light," he summed up these earlier

[6]Ibid., 14:77–79.
[7]"The 'Miscellanies,' no. 331," WJE, 13:409.
[8]"The 'Miscellanies,' no. 263," WJE, 13:369–70.

thoughts and put them in definitive statement. Even more, this sermon provides an important understanding of how God applies redemption to us individually. This glorious story of redemption—which moves from creation to new creation through the cross of Jesus—is applied to individuals when God works immediately in their hearts so that they are able to see and feel, they are able to taste and believe. So affected, men and women reflect God's light to the world, living out of the glory of this redemption in new ways of charity, worship, and obedience for God's glory, until either Jesus returns or they die looking to Jesus.

Spiritual Knowledge

Edwards's sermon was based on Matthew 16:17, in which Jesus tells Simon Peter that the spiritual knowledge that Jesus is "Christ, the Son of the living God," was granted to him by God. In fact, such knowledge was not something that "flesh and blood" could reveal at all. Spiritual knowledge "is what God is the author of, and none else: he reveals it, and flesh and blood reveals it not. He imparts this knowledge immediately, not making use of any intermediate natural causes, as he does in other knowledge." Here at the beginning of the sermon, Edwards set forward his key points: God is the author of spiritual knowledge; he imparts this knowledge immediately; such knowledge affects the individual; and God does this to stress his sovereignty and magnify his glory.[9]

Edwards distinguished spiritual knowledge from the knowledge that natural or unconverted men and women have. People in a lost or natural condition may have "convictions." They may know something about the possibility of divine vengeance and divine anger. In fact, such conviction might even come from God's Spirit; but this is only the Spirit "assisting natural principles, and not as infusing any new principles." Edwards called this "common grace": "it influences only by assisting of nature, and not

---

[9]Jonathan Edwards, "A Divine and Supernatural Light," in *WJE*, vol. 17, *Sermons and Discourses, 1730–1733*, ed. Mark Valeri (New Haven, CT: Yale University Press, 1999), 409.

by imparting grace, or bestowing anything above nature." When the Spirit imparts special grace, he causes a new "principle of nature" to exist in the soul so that the individual's mind "habitually" exerts itself in obedience to God's Word. Indeed, the Spirit "acts in the mind of a saint as an indwelling vital principle" and "communicates" himself to the saint so that he might live holily as the Spirit of God is holy.[10]

Moreover, spiritual knowledge is not an "impression made upon the imagination." This divine light is not an actual light that impresses itself on the mind's eye. It is not a vision of divine glory, a dream of Christ's light, or a sense of angelic presence. People may experience these sensations, but there is no guarantee that these are holy lights. After all, the Bible tells us that the Devil can transform himself into "an angel of light" (2 Cor. 11:14). But such impressions are far below what the Bible teaches about this divine and supernatural light.[11]

In addition, spiritual knowledge is not the suggestion of any "new truths" or propositions not contained in Scripture. It is not "new light" breaking forth from Scripture that contradicts Scripture or a "spiritual light" that comes alongside and supplements Scripture. Further, spiritual knowledge is not an emotional response to religious truth or spiritual rhetoric. "Men by mere principles of nature are capable of being affected with things that have a special relation to religion, as well as other things," Edwards noted. People might be affected by the story of Jesus and especially his self-sacrifice, the blessedness of heaven, the joy of the saints, or the glories of God. But this is nothing more to them than having their "imagination be entertained by a romantic description of the pleasantness of a fairyland." None of these things represents spiritual knowledge.[12]

For Edwards, spiritual knowledge is "a true sense of the divine excellency of the things revealed in the Word of God, and a conviction of the truth and reality of them, thence arising." "Sense"

[10]Ibid., 17:410, 411.
[11]Ibid., 17:412.
[12]Ibid.

is an important Edwardsian word: it will come up again in his *Religious Affections*. By it, Edwards drew on a distinction from eighteenth-century philosopher John Locke between "speculative" knowledge and "sensible" knowledge. All real knowing—or perhaps better, every building block of real knowing—comes through sensation. As we experience sensations, our minds organize those sensations and reflect on their meaning; those connections that our minds make represent a second-order kind of knowing, a more reflective or speculative kind.[13]

A few sentences after this basic definition of spiritual knowledge, Edwards makes explicit his distinction between speculative and sensible knowing:

> There is a twofold understanding or knowledge of good, that God has made the mind of man capable of. The first, that which is merely speculative or notional: as when a person only speculatively judges, that anything is, which by the agreement of mankind, is called good or excellent, viz. that which is most to general advantage, and between which and reward there is a suitableness; and the like. And the other is that which consists in the sense of the heart: as when there is a sense of the beauty, amiableness, or sweetness of a thing; so that the heart is sensible of pleasure and delight in the presence of the idea of it.

While it would be simplistic to pit speculative and sensible knowledge against one another as the battle between the head and the heart, still there is a privileging of a type of "heart" knowing that is more basic than "head" knowing. As Edwards put it, "He that is spiritually enlightened truly apprehends and sees it, or has a sense of it. He don't merely rationally believe that God is glorious, but he has a sense of the gloriousness of God in his heart." And this heart sense of God's glorious nature draws out affections that move the will to obey God's Word and ways. Thus,

---

[13]Ibid., 17:413; John Locke, *An Essay Concerning Human Understanding* (New York: Oxford University Press, 1964), 273. For Edwards's use of Locke in framing his own theory of knowing, see Sang Hyun Lee, *The Philosophical Theology of Jonathan Edwards* (Princeton, NJ: Princeton University Press, 1988), 117–25.

in saying that spiritual knowledge involves sensation and that of a particular kind, Edwards claimed that true spiritual knowing is not merely "rational" or "intellectual." Spiritual knowing is not simply intellectually crunching and organizing doctrinal propositions found in Scripture. It involves sensible response to the divine excellency of those scriptural truths, which in turn leads to conviction about their truth and reality.[14]

This statement about spiritual knowledge is important also for having a true sense of divine excellency. Again, "excellency" is another important word in Edwards's lexicon. In his early twenties, Edwards explored a range of philosophical concepts, one of which was excellency, and, importantly, his exploration of the topic showed up in a notebook "The Mind." As a result, excellency was basic to his understanding of how the mind and knowing work, which impacted his understanding of how we know God.

For Edwards, excellency has its roots in spatial dimensions such as harmony, symmetry, and proportion, which communicate equality, but cannot simply be identified with these things. Rather, equality is important because it coheres with our understandings of "beauty." And so, "simple equality . . . may be called simple beauty; all other beauties and excellencies may be resolved into it. Proportion is complex beauty." While Edwards went on to demonstrate this in his notebooks, we must not miss what he was saying: excellency represents a kind of beauty; it is an aesthetic judgment rooted in an understanding of the harmony or fitness between two (or more) things.[15]

Returning to Edwards's understanding of spiritual knowledge: it is a true sense of the divine excellency of the things revealed in the Word of God. That is, spiritual knowledge is a deep, basic sensation of the divine beauty, proportion, fitness of things revealed in Scripture. However, there is one more thing: spiritual knowledge in this fashion is not a bare drudgery or forced consent. Not at all. "When the heart is sensible of the beauty and amiableness

---

[14]"A Divine and Supernatural Light," *WJE*, 17:413.
[15]Jonathan Edwards, "The Mind," in *WJE*, 6:332–38 (no. 1).

of a thing, it necessarily feels pleasure in the apprehension. It is implied in a person's being heartily sensible of the loveliness of a thing, that the idea of it is sweet and pleasant to his soul." There is a fundamental delight that comes to us when we gain spiritual knowledge—not delight in ourselves, but delight in the object of our knowing because it appears beautiful and lovely to us.[16]

This delightful, sensible knowing produces a conviction of the truth and reality of those things revealed in God's Word—that they are worthy of trust. Old prejudices against the truth found in Scripture seem to fall away or to be no longer relevant or important. Even more, because of this divine knowing, spiritual mental muscles seem to be more "lively" because the mind is now working along with the fabric of God's Word and world rather than against it. Now there is a delight to meditate on divine revelation, which gives a truer picture of the world and human life in it than that gained from reason alone. And the result is a deepening conviction that the propositions of Scripture are true and spiritual. That, said Edwards, is "saving faith."[17]

Spiritually Imparted

While God uses "means" to impart spiritual knowledge, this divine sense is not dependent upon those means as though they somehow cause it. Certainly, Edwards argued, God uses his Word. In fact, this divine and supernatural light "is not given without the Word." But that is a far cry from saying that the Word by itself gives the light.

> Indeed a person can't have spiritual light without the Word. But that don't argue, that the Word properly causes that light. The mind can't see the excellency of any doctrine, unless that doctrine be first in the mind; but the seeing the excellency of the doctrine may be immediately from the Spirit; though the conveying of the doctrine or proposition itself may be by the Word. So that the notions that are the subject matter of this

---

[16]"A Divine and Supernatural Light," *WJE*, 17:414.
[17]Ibid., 17:415.

light, are conveyed to the mind by the Word of God; but that due sense of the heart, wherein this light formally consists, is immediately by the Spirit of God.

Word and Spirit are glued together tightly, but Edwards will never let one forget that it is God the Holy Spirit who, without any mediation, gives the light to our hearts.[18]

While such an emphasis upon the Spirit's working serves as a salutary corrective to humans' implicit rationalism, it doesn't do away with the need for the Word. If spiritual knowledge involves a genuine sense of the holy beauty of things in Scripture, then we must know intellectually those things in Scripture. We cannot see the excellency of things about which we know nothing. Thus, Edwards certainly provided a place for our *heads* in the Christian life; he expected us to think. And yet, rationalization only has a limited value; it can perceive truth, but it cannot perceive beauty. Without the new sense of the heart given immediately by God the Spirit, such speculative knowledge can only serve to damn.[19]

Light and Heat

Light does not simply bring illumination; it also brings heat. The linking together of light and heat is a common occurrence in Edwards's writing and serves to ensure that this image for spiritual knowledge does not devolve into the merely speculative. For example, Edwards observed early in *Religious Affections*:

> As there is no true religion, where there is nothing else but affection; so there is no true religion where there is no religious affection. As on the one hand, there must be light in the understanding, as well as an affected fervent heart, where there is heat without light, there can be nothing divine or heavenly in that heart; so on the other hand, where there is a kind of light without heat, a head stored with notions and speculations, with a cold and unaffected heart, there can be nothing divine in that light, that knowledge is no true spiritual knowledge of divine things.

---

[18]Ibid., 17:416–17.
[19]Ibid., 17:422.

Light and heat belong together in order for there to be true spiritual knowing; speculative and sensible knowledge moves the affections and produces genuine holiness.[20]

And so, "heat" in the Edwardsian parlance equates to holy actions, and these holy actions will manifest themselves in practical acts of love. Edwards preached in his sermons on "Charity and Its Fruits":

> Love is no ingredient in a merely speculative faith; but it is the life and soul of a practical faith. A truly practical and saving faith is light and heat together, or light and love. That which is only a speculative, is only light without heat. But in that it wants spiritual heat or divine love, it is vain and good for nothing. A speculative faith consists only in assent; but in a saving faith are assent and consent together.

Notice how Edwards's themes come together here: saving faith is light and heat together, sensible knowing and transformed affections. Speculative faith is really speculative knowing—it is only "assent," only rationalization of or reflection upon ideas. But saving faith is both rational knowing (assent) and sensible knowing of excellency (consent; think proportion, harmony, and equality here, the consent of the parts to the whole).

Now we must come back again to how the light/heat imagery relates to the very nature and communication of the Trinity. Twice in his "Miscellanies," Edwards related the imagery of light and heat to God's own being. Relating the Trinity to the sun, he claimed, "The Father is as the substance of the sun; the Son is as the brightness and glory of the disk of the sun; the Holy Ghost is as the heat and continually emitted influence, the emanation by which the world is enlightened, warmed, enlivened and comforted." God himself shines his light through the Son and communicates his heat by the Spirit; in this way, he emanates or communicates himself to his creation. Again, in "Miscellanies," no. 370, Edwards affirmed

---

[20]Jonathan Edwards, *WJE*, vol. 2, *Religious Affections*, ed. John E. Smith (New Haven, CT: Yale University Press, 1959), 120.

the same parallels between the Trinity and the sun and explained further that "the Spirit, as it is God's infinite love and happiness, is as the internal heat of the sun; but as it is that by which God communicates himself, is as the emitted beams of God's glory." Again, the Spirit is related to the heat of the sun, but he is more; he is God's infinite love and happiness. When God communicates himself immediately to the soul, grants genuine spiritual knowledge, produces a sensible knowing of the beauty of divine things revealed in Scripture, creates a holy conviction about the truth and reality of these things, and produces a delight and relish of these things—when God the Holy Spirit does this, he is communicating his own self, his own love, his own happiness in himself.[21]

So it is that ultimately, the imparting of this divine light is at the center of God's purpose for the world. As Edwards put it in this 1731 sermon,

> 'Tis rational to suppose that this blessing should be immediately from God; for there is no gift or benefit that is itself so nearly related to the divine nature, there is nothing the creature receives that is so much of God, of his nature, so much a participation of the Deity: 'tis a kind of emanation of God's beauty, and is related to God as the light is to the sun.

That word "emanation" is an important clue: it connects us to Edwards's treatise *The End for Which God Created the World*. God's purpose in this world is to pour out his light into the lives of his creation so that they might reflect that light back to him. The philosophical language of "emanation" and "remanation" speaks to this capacious vision.[22]

This reflection of light is not merely rational; it is affectional. God grants his people spiritual knowledge so that they might delight and rejoice and love him. The light is accompanied by heat, spiritual knowing with spiritual affections. And the end is love.

---

[21] "The 'Miscellanies,' no. 362," *WJE*, 13:434; "The 'Miscellanies,' no. 370," *WJE*, 13:411.
[22] "A Divine and Supernatural Light," *WJE*, 17:422.

CHAPTER 6

The Nature of True Religion

Holy Affections

Most people who know something about Jonathan Edwards know that his most important book was *A Treatise Concerning Religious Affections*. Published in 1746, it was originally a sermon series, based on 1 Peter 1:8, preached to Edwards's Northampton congregation during the winter of 1742–1743. That timing was important: the first sermonic version was delivered right at the end of the Great Awakening as Edwards was sorting through the pastoral effects of the revival.

Even more important was his purpose. In the sermons, Edwards dealt with the spiritual pride and apathy within his congregation after the awakening. As he later related to a Scottish correspondent, Thomas Gillespie, Edwards worried that the congregation was rife with spiritual arrogance.

89

The people . . . are become more extensively famous in the world, as a people that have excelled in gifts and grace, and had God extraordinarily among them: which has insensibly engendered and nourished spiritual pride, that grand inlet of the Devil into the hearts of men, and avenue of all manner of mischief among a professing people.

Of course, the way Northampton became famous in evangelical circles was through Edwards's own writing about the awakening of 1734–1735. He expressed to Gillespie, "There is this inconvenience [that] attends the publishing of narratives of a work of God among a people: such is the corruption that is in the hearts of men, and even of good men, that there is great danger of their making it an occasion of spiritual pride." As pride crept into the congregation, people became satisfied with their spiritual attainments and left off pursuing hard after God. Apathy was the result.[1]

Edwards had a second concern that led him to preach the sermons that became *Religious Affections*. As he put it memorably, "Another thing that evidently has contributed to our calamities is, that the people had got so established in certain wrong notions and ways in religion, which I found them in and never could beat them out of."[2] In particular, the Northampton congregation had two sets of "wrong notions." The first wrong notion was laying

almost all the stress of their hopes on the particular steps and method of their first work, i.e. the first work of the Spirit of God on their hearts in their convictions and conversion, and to look but little at the abiding sense and temper of their hearts, and the course of their exercises, and fruits of grace, for evidences of their good estates.

---

[1] Jonathan Edwards to Thomas Gillespie, July 1, 1751, in *The Works of Jonathan Edwards* (hereafter *WJE*), vol. 4, *The Great Awakening*, ed. C. C. Goen (New Haven, CT: Yale University Press, 1972), 563. Several paragraphs of this chapter draw from Sean Michael Lucas, "'What Is the Nature of True Religion?': *Religious Affections* and its American Puritan Context," in *All for Jesus: A Celebration of the 50th Anniversary of Covenant Theological Seminary*, ed. R. A. Peterson and S. M. Lucas (Ross-Faire, UK: Christian Focus, 2006).
[2] Edwards to Gillespie, July 1, 1751, *WJE*, 4:564.

For generations, New England Calvinists had sought salvation according to particular steps: moving from preparation through conviction and humiliation to closing with Christ. Evidentially, Northampton believers had the same mind-set, which meant that they put more stress on the steps to salvation than on the evidence of God's grace in their lives.[3]

The second wrong notion was Northampton believers' inability "to distinguish between impressions on the imagination, and truly spiritual experiences." When Edwards came to Northampton in 1727 to serve as an assistant minister for his grandfather Solomon Stoddard, he found people ready "to declare and publish their own experience; and oftentimes to do it in a light manner, without any air of solemnity." As he worked with the congregation, he became increasingly convinced that much of their spiritual growth that occurred during the revivals was ephemeral. What many had taken for conversion was actually impressions on the imagination accompanied by bodily effects and not truly spiritual experience. As a result, a large number of his congregation was spiritually deceived.[4]

After Edwards had preached the sermons, though, there was a published challenge to the awakening—its benefits, reality, and success. Early in 1743, Charles Chauncy, pastor of First Church, Boston, and leader of the protoliberal "Old Lights," produced *Seasonable Thoughts on the State of Religion in New England*. Chauncy argued that the social effects of the awakening—which produced all types of moral license—demonstrated that it was no "work of God." Chauncy's book provided Edwards an additional referent as he transformed his sermons into a treatise.[5]

---

[3]Edwards to Gillespie, July 1, 1751, *WJE*, 4:564. For more on what some scholars call "the morphology of conversion," see Norman Petit, *The Heart Prepared: Grace and Conversion in Puritan Spiritual Life*, 2nd ed. (Middletown, CT: Wesleyan University Press, 1989).

[4]Edwards to Gillespie, July 1, 1751, *WJE*, 4:564.

[5]Charles Chauncy, *Seasonable Thoughts on the State of Religion in New England* (Boston: Rogers and Fowle, 1743). See also Amy Schranger Lang, "'A Flood of Errors': Chauncy and Edwards in the Great Awakening," in *Jonathan Edwards and the American Experience*, ed. Nathan Hatch and Harry Stout (New York: Oxford University Press, 1988), 160–73.

With these two contexts in mind—his own congregation's spiritual pride, apathy, and confused notions about true religion, alongside Chauncy's evident misunderstanding about genuine spiritual life—Edwards slowly worked to transform his sermons into a book. As he did, he continued to work with an idea that "true religion, in great part, consists in holy affections."[6]

Affections

What did Edwards mean by "affections"? That is not an easy question. All too often, people suggest that he meant something close to emotions. But affections are not exactly emotions; rather, Edwards said that "the affections are no other, than the more vigorous and sensible exercises of the inclination and will of the soul." Likewise, affections are not "passions." In eighteenth-century philosophical parlance, passions were irrational and out-of-control emotions that were to be avoided at all costs; and affections were not irrational, but rational, deeper springs of action. To understand what this means, one needs to step back and understand a little bit of how Edwards thought about being, the philosophical commitments we call ontology.[7]

For Edwards, in order for something to have being or existence, understanding and will are required.[8] And this being—summed up in the interplay between understanding and will—finds its expression in habit or disposition. As philosophical theologian Sang Hyun Lee has explained, habits are not thoughtless ways in which actions are carried out; rather, "the habit of mind, for Edwards, functions as the very possibility of rationality and moral action." Edwards held that

all habits [are] only a law that God has fixed that such actions upon such occasions should be exerted. . . . So in the first birth

---

[6]Jonathan Edwards, *WJE*, vol. 2, *Religious Affections*, ed. John E. Smith (New Haven, CT: Yale University Press, 1959), 95.
[7]Ibid., 2:96. On the passions, see David Walker Howe, *Making the American Self: From Jonathan Edwards to Abraham Lincoln* (Cambridge: Harvard University Press, 1997).
[8]Edwards defined human beings this way in *Religious Affections*, *WJE*, 2:96, and God's being in "Discourse on the Trinity," in *WJE*, vol. 21, *Writings on the Trinity, Grace, and Faith*, ed. Sang Hyun Lee (New Haven, CT: Yale University Press, 2003), 134.

it seems to me probable that the beginning of the existence of the soul, whose essence consists in powers and habits, is with some kind of new alteration there, either in motion or sensation.

That is to say that human existence, human *being*, consists in habits or dispositions that act when there is some motion or sensation brought to bear upon them. Or, to use the language of Lee, "Habit is, rather, an active tendency that governs and brings about certain types of events and actions."[9]

It is important to recognize that Edwards used other words to stand in for habit or disposition, including *inclination, temper, principle of nature*, and *sense of the heart*. So when he defines the affections as "the more vigorous and sensible exercises of *the inclination* and will of the soul," it is the same thing as saying that the *affections are the exercises of habit or disposition that have been moved to act by sensation*. That definition, rightly understood, is key for grasping what Edwards was saying about the Christian life.[10]

Still, Edwards was careful to note that not all affections are positive, nor are they all vigorous. As the understanding and will evaluate certain sensations, there will be reactions: approval or disapproval, approbation or disapprobation. Sometimes the approval or disapproval is such that the individual is largely indifferent; he is not affected by the sensation in a way that moves him to action. But at other times, the sensation affects someone to such a degree that one's body is engaged and one's will acts decisively. It is also important to say that the will and the affections are not separate. Rather, the affections are better thought of as a set of vigorous reactions to sensation or stimuli that bring about the will's exercise. If the will remains in a state of indifference, then one can say that it is "unaffected."[11]

---

[9]Sang Hyun Lee, *The Philosophical Theology of Jonathan Edwards* (Princeton, NJ: Princeton University Press, 1988), 8, 35; Jonathan Edwards, "The 'Miscellanies,' no. 241," in *WJE*, vol. 13, *The "Miscellanies," a–500*, ed. Thomas A. Schafer (New Haven, CT: Yale University Press, 1994), 358.
[10]Lee, *Philosophical Theology of Jonathan Edwards*, 15.
[11]*Religious Affections*, *WJE*, 2:96–97.

Now, all of this simply speaks to the nature of affections. It does not yet get someone to a "religious affection," but it seems obvious how Edwards would use this understanding. True religion—real, vital, biblical Christianity—consists in the movement of one's will toward obedience to God. But how does that happen? The will moves toward obedience only when and insofar as it is affected. And when a spiritual or religious sensation brings about an exercise of one's will (or habit, disposition, or inclination) so that the individual obeys God, that is a *holy affection*.

Even more, if an individual professes faith in Jesus, but does not evidence the regular exercise of the will so that there are new spiritual practices and attitudes that conform to Scripture and does not display a "fervent, vigorous engagedness of the heart in religion," then there should be a legitimate question whether or not there is real spiritual life. "That religion which God requires, and will accept," Edwards observed, "does not consist in weak, dull and lifeless wouldings, raising us but a little above a state of indifference: God, in his Word, greatly insists upon it, that we be in good earnest, fervent in spirit, and our hearts vigorously engaged in religion." As our hearts are affected, the will moves to engage in holy practices—this is true religion. But if not, "if we ben't in good earnest in religion, and our wills and inclinations be not strongly exercised, we are nothing."[12]

And so, fervent, vigorous, and habitual movements of the soul that produce holy practices characterize the Christian life. Some of these affections include godly fear, hope in God and in his Word, love to God and the people of God, holy hatred for sin, holy desire for God and holiness, holy joy, religious sorrow and mourning, gratitude and praise to God, compassion and mercy, and holy zeal. However, of all these affections, the greatest is love. Edwards called love "the chief of the affections and fountain of all other affections." In fact, "the essence of all true religion lies in holy love," and love sums "the whole of religion."[13]

---

[12]Ibid., 2:99.

[13]See Edwards's description of each of these in ibid., 2:102–7. The quotations on love are found on p. 107. The language about habit is found on pp. 118–19. Edwards's

The problem for the Christian life is that all human beings are sinners pervaded with guilt and corruption from Adam's fall. Because Adam lost original righteousness, which for Edwards was the restraining and directing activity of the Holy Spirit, Adam and all his posterity are left with the disposition or inclination toward self-love. As a result, all people seek their own way, worship their desires as gods, find their disposition bent toward selfish and destructive ends, and exercise love for themselves. The sinful heart is a hardened heart, insensible to God's glory and excellency and not easily moved to spiritual affections. Not only this, but a sinful, hardened heart is also susceptible to other, unholy affections: hatred, anger, and arrogance. And these unholy affections produce unholy actions and evidence a state of spiritual death.[14]

New Sense of the Heart

Clearly, then, if someone is going to have holy affections, he will need a new disposition no longer bent on or inclined toward self-love as its greatest good, but bent on or inclined toward love for God as its greatest good. The only way an individual can receive a new disposition is through "the special, gracious and saving influences of God's Spirit." The Holy Spirit dwells in the souls of believers "to influence their hearts, as a principle of new nature, or as a divine supernatural spring of life and action." He is united to the understanding and the will so that the believer gains a new disposition, inclination, and temper of mind.[15]

By virtue of this divine communication, the believer is drawn into the Trinitarian life: "The saint has truly fellowship with the Father, and with his Son Jesus Christ, in thus having the communion or participation of the Holy Ghost." While the Spirit does not communicate his own proper nature, so that believers are somehow "'Godded' with God or 'Christed' with Christ," yet the Spirit does enable saints to have "a participation of God."

observation here will prove important for understanding *Charity and Its Fruits*, as well as *The Nature of True Virtue*.

[14]*Religious Affections*, WJE, 2:116–18.

[15]Ibid., 2:199, 200.

Believers partake of God's spiritual beauty and happiness according to their finite capacities, they experience the goodness of God, and God truly communicates himself to the believer.[16]

Above all, God's Spirit enters the souls of saints and grants "a new inward perception or sensation of their minds, entirely different in its nature and kind, from anything that ever their minds were the subjects of before they were sanctified." That language of sensation is important: remember that when a spiritual or religious sensation brings about an exercise of one's will (or habit, disposition, or inclination) so that the individual obeys God, that is a holy affection. What Edwards, then, was saying is this: the Spirit enters into the soul of the individual so that he or she is able to experience new, holy sensations or perceptions that so affect the individual—with love, fear, desire, zeal, and so forth—that he or she acts out in new, holy ways.[17]

The Spirit conveys this "new spiritual sense" or "new sense of the heart," but it is a new disposition or inclination, not a new faculty (like understanding or will). Older theologians confessed that the Spirit works to call sinners to God by "enlightening their minds spiritually and savingly to understand the things of God, taking away their heart of stone, and giving unto them a heart of flesh; [and] renewing their wills." Edwards was saying the same thing: the Spirit must first "infuse" a new spiritual principle or disposition, namely himself, so that a sinner can perceive and sense rightly; then, as the Word is preached, the individual senses the glory of God and excellency of Christ in such a way that the heart is affected and the will is engaged to act in holy obedience.[18]

As the believer begins to exercise this new disposition, he finds that other internal changes begin to develop. As a result of the new sense of the heart, he is enabled to love God in a disinterested manner. Edwards insisted that the new spiritual sense provides "the first foundation of a true love to God" found

---

[16]Ibid., 2:201, 203.
[17]Ibid., 2:205.
[18]Ibid., 2:206, 207 ("infuse"), 209 ("excellency"); Westminster Confession of Faith 10.1.

in "the supreme loveliness of his nature." Saints "first see that God is lovely, and that Christ is excellent and glorious, and their hearts are first captivated with this view." Such a sight of God's excellency, beauty, and holiness is a result of this new sense of the heart. And the response of love returning back to God, loving God for God's own sake, is the first act of a new heart.[19]

The new spiritual sense also produces a new understanding. Edwards reminded his readers that

> holy affections are not heat without light; but evermore arise from some information of the understanding, some spiritual instruction that the mind receives, some light or actual knowledge. The child of God is graciously affected, because he sees and understands something more of divine things than he did before.[20]

He argued that this new spiritual understanding

> consists in a sense of the heart, of the supreme beauty and sweetness of the holiness or moral perfection of divine things, together with all that discerning and knowledge of things of religion, that depends upon, and flows from such a sense. Spiritual understanding consists primarily in a sense of heart of that spiritual beauty.

The new sense of the heart "opens a new world to its view" so that the perfections and beauty of God are seen, perhaps for the first time, in his creation, in his Word, and in his saints.[21]

And so, this new sense of the heart is a new disposition that enables someone to see the beauty and excellency of Jesus in a

---

[19]*Religious Affections*, WJE, 2:241, 242, 246. Further on, Edwards wrote, "The first foundation of the delight a true saint has in God, is his own perfection; and the first foundation of the delight he has in Christ, is his own beauty; he appears in himself the chief among ten thousand, and altogether lovely. . . . They first have their hearts filled with sweetness, from the view of Christ's excellency, and the excellency of his grace, and the beauty of the way of salvation by him; and then they have a secondary joy, in that so excellent a Savior, and such excellent grace as theirs" (ibid., 250).
[20]*Religious Affections*, WJE, 2:266.
[21]Ibid., 2:272, 273.

way that he never saw before. This new disposition, or inclination or affection, is not divorced from knowledge, but profoundly connected with spiritual understanding and knowledge. As the Spirit uses his Word to show the individual Christ's beauty, the individual moves toward Jesus in faith. It is also important, at this point, to connect the dots between "a divine and supernatural light" and "holy affections." This divine and supernatural light that is communicated to the soul immediately is nothing less than the Spirit of God himself, infused into the soul, so that spiritual knowledge is the result. Remember that spiritual knowledge is "sensible" knowing. And here is the connection: the new sense of the heart is sensible knowing as well; there is a new way of seeing God and his excellency; there is a new, spiritual knowledge; and it all produces different ways of living. Light produces heat.

True Signs of God's Work

As this new sense, this new disposition, which is nothing less than the Holy Spirit, continues to animate the choices of the individual, there will be several signs that God is at work.

Gracious Gratitude

One sign is what Edwards calls "a gracious gratitude, which does greatly differ from all that gratitude which natural men experience." This gratitude is primarily toward God and arises from a love for God "for what he is in himself," as opposed to what God can do or has done for me. As the believer lives in response to this new disposition in his heart, he finds delight in meditating on God's glorious character; and this delight expresses itself in gratitude for who God is and what God has done. In other words, the new sense expresses itself in disinterested benevolence to God and others.[22]

Delight in Holiness

Another sign that God is at work transforming the individual is a new longing for and delight in holiness. "Holy persons, in the

---

[22]Ibid., 2:247.

exercise of holy affections, do love things primarily for their holiness." Certainly such a delight in holiness will focus particularly on God's own holiness. Edwards noted that "a true love for God must begin with a delight in his holiness and not with a delight in any other attribute." Believers begin to develop a taste and relish for the sweetness of God's holiness and an equal distaste and hatred of sin, which would become increasingly bitter to them. They will be enabled "to determine what actions are right and becoming Christians, not only more speedily, but far more exactly" than before, this because of the Spirit of God indwelling them and the new sense of the heart acting as a new disposition.[23]

Evangelical Humility

A third sign that God is at work in granting new affections to an individual is an evangelical humility that pervades his or her life. Edwards held that "evangelical humiliation is a sense that a Christian has of his own utter insufficiency, despicableness, and odiousness, with an answerable frame of heart." This sense comes from "the special influences of the Spirit of God, implanting and exercising supernatural and divine principles" in the life of the individual. Again, this is the "new sense of the heart" or the new holy affections of the soul. True religion will always be accompanied by evangelical humility, Edwards believed. And this is because such humility is "from a sense of the transcendent beauty of divine things in the moral qualities" and from "a discovery of the beauty of God's holiness and moral perfection." Such a sense rebukes all spiritual pride and discovers sin in every intent and action.[24]

Holy Practices

But the most important sign of God's work is an individual's new holy practices. If God the Holy Spirit truly indwells the individual, if there is actually a new disposition or new sense of the heart, then there will inevitably be new practices of holiness as a result. "Grace and holy affections have their exercise and

---

[23]Ibid., 2:256, 257, 260, 283.
[24]Ibid., 2:311, 312, 325.

fruit in Christian practice," Edwards said. "I mean, they have that influence and power upon him who is the subject of 'em, that they cause that practice, which is universally conformed to, and directed by Christian rules should be the practice and business of his life." And this is because the power of godliness "chiefly appears . . . in its being effectual in practice." Godliness does not simply remain in the heart as a private faith; rather, godliness is principally evidenced "in those exercises of holy affections that are practical, and in their being practical; in conquering the will, and conquering the lusts and corruptions of men, and carrying men on in the way of holiness, through all temptation, difficulty, and opposition."[25]

Such Christian obedience will be universal in its extent. That is to say, an individual who has a new disposition to love God and his holiness will not be satisfied with holy practice in one area, only to neglect it in another. Rather, he declares war on little as well as big sins; in every area of life, the desire is to become more like Jesus. Moreover, such growth in Christian obedience will be "the main business" of the believer's life, one that persists through every season of life regardless the trials he might meet. That is because the "fruit of holy practice, is what every grace, and every discovery, and every individual thing, which belongs to Christian experience, has a direct tendency to."[26]

This understanding of true religion consisting in holy affections would be the standard by which Edwards would judge what he saw in the Great Awakening. While there was much in his congregation and the evangelical community that frustrated him, he still was hopeful that the divine and supernatural light that was shining, and the new spiritual sense that was being granted, would prove effectual in the end. After all, if Christians lived holy lives, lives marked by light and heat, new affections and new practice, then

[25]Ibid., 2:383, 393.
[26]Ibid., 2:384, 388–89, 399. Edwards quotes his grandfather, Solomon Stoddard: "If a man lives in small sins, that shews he has no love to God, no sincere care to please and honor God. Little sins are of a damning nature, as well as great: if they don't deserve so much punishment as greater, yet they do deserve damnation" (ibid., 385n8).

a great many of the main stumbling blocks against experimental and powerful religion would be removed; and religion would be declared and manifested in such a way, that instead of hardening spectators, and exceedingly promoting infidelity and atheism, would above all things tend to convince men that there is a reality in religion, and greatly awaken them, and win them, by convincing their consciences of the importance and excellency of religion.

Fittingly, the last words in *Religious Affections* take us back toward the image of light: "Thus the light of professors would so shine before men, that others seeing their good works, would glorify their Father which is in heaven."[27]

---

[27]Ibid., 2:461.

CHAPTER 7

The Dark Side of
Religious Affections

Self-Deception

T hough many people are familiar with at least some of
Edwards's argument in *Religious Affections*, they are probably unaware that there is another, darker side to what he
was saying. Once again, recognizing the larger context is helpful.
The Great Awakening, both in 1734–1735 and in 1739–1742,
was spiritually messy, culturally overwhelming, and even politi-
cally charged. Itinerant ministers, convinced that the local parish
ministers were "unconverted," would come into those parishes
and pulpits to preach awakening sermons. Likewise, as Presbyterians and Congregationalists divided over the awakening,
there were differences not only over doctrine and practice, but
also over individual choice versus community traditions. Some

scholars believe the latter difference contributed to an emerging American consciousness that would explode in 1775.[1]

But the spiritual, cultural, and political converged in the emergence of a New Light style of religion that embraced an emotional response to preaching, unusual physical displays, immediate divine communication, and ardent attachment to charismatic personalities. Perhaps the great example of this confluence and these reactions can be found in the hysteria that accompanied the ministry of James Davenport. Ordained in 1738 in Southold, Long Island, Davenport became enamored of the preaching of popular revivalists George Whitefield and Gilbert Tennent. In 1741, Davenport decided to become an itinerant and immediately drew notice as a fiery preacher, charismatic leader, and heated controversialist. He encouraged people to seek immediate communications from God, believed that he could discern who was saved and who was not, and denounced ministers as unconverted or worse whom he believed to be lost. He also led people in burning various "immoral" books and luxuries as signs of their commitment to God. Finally, in 1743, Davenport went too far: at one particular bonfire, he urged people to throw luxurious clothing into the fire and he took the lead by pulling off his pants and throwing them to the flames. A woman retrieved them for him and urged him to come back to his senses. Such excess discredited Davenport's ministry and raised questions about his followers' spiritual condition.[2]

During and after the awakening, Edwards was at great pains to distinguish between true revival and conversion and false. He devoted a sermon at Yale College's 1741 commencement to pointing out "distinguishing marks of a work of the Spirit of God." And, as already noted, the burden of *Religious Affections* was to

---

[1]Timothy Hall, *Contested Boundaries: Itinerancy and the Reshaping of the Colonial American Religious World* (Durham, NC: Duke University Press, 1994); Alan Heimert, *Religion and the American Mind: From the Great Awakening to the Revolution* (Cambridge: Harvard University Press, 1966).
[2]On Davenport, see Thomas Kidd, *The Great Awakening: The Roots of Evangelical Christianity in Colonial America* (New Haven, CT: Yale University Press, 2007), 138–55; Harry S. Stout, *The New England Soul: Preaching and Religious Culture in Colonial America* (New York: Oxford University Press, 1986), 197–202.

mark out what true revival and conversion look like. However, what must be recognized is that Edwards also sought to identify the characteristics of false religion; or to put it differently, he attempted to show colonial men and women that they very well might have been self-deceived about their spiritual condition.[3]

This possibility of self-deception represents both the darker side of *Religious Affections* and a remarkably realistic pastoral understanding. While some eighteenth-century Protestant traditions attempted to account for the problem of apostasy by holding that people might "lose their salvation," Edwards instead recognized that, pastorally speaking, those who confidently professed their faith during the halcyon days of the awakening might actually have been self-deceived. Those who were and knew themselves to be spiritually lost were relatively obvious: "He who has no religious affection, is in a state of spiritual death, and is wholly destitute of the powerful, quickening, saving influences of God upon his heart," Edwards stated. The problem was that during the awakening period, discerning what were true, holy affections and what were spurious ones was difficult. "There are false affections, and there are true. A man's having much affection, don't prove that he has any true religion: but if he has no affection, it proves that he has no true religion," Edwards wrote. "The right way, is not to reject all affections, nor to approve all; but to distinguish between affections, approving some, and rejecting others; separating between the wheat and the chaff, the gold and the dross, the precious and the vile."[4]

The need to distinguish between true and false affections was necessary because the awakening brought powerful sensations to bear on the minds, hearts, and wills of colonials. And these sensations could move the affections in ways that looked truly spiritual. Edwards put it this way:

[3]Jonathan Edwards, "The Distinguishing Marks of a Work of the Spirit of God," in *The Works of Jonathan Edwards* (hereafter *WJE*), vol. 4, *The Great Awakening*, ed. C. C. Goen (New Haven, CT: Yale University Press, 1972), 213–88; Ava Chamberlain, "Self-deception as a Theological Problem in Jonathan Edwards's 'Treatise concerning Religious Affections,'" *Church History* 63 (1994): 541–56.
[4]Jonathan Edwards, *WJE*, vol. 2, *Religious Affections*, ed. John E. Smith (New Haven, CT: Yale University Press, 1959), 120, 121.

A natural man may have those religious apprehensions and affections, which may be in many respects very new and surprising to him, and what before he did not conceive of; and yet what he experiences be nothing like the exercises of a principle of new nature, or the sensations of a new spiritual sense.

In fact, such an individual might experience affections that are new, extraordinary, and heightened, producing new ideas and even new behavior for a time. And yet, all this would simply be "extraordinarily raising and exciting natural principles . . . ; here is nothing like giving him a new sense."[5]

Thus, what was required, and what Edwards attempted to do in *Religious Affections*, was to identify both true and false affections. While true affections are granted by the work of the indwelling Holy Spirit, who is infused into the heart of the believer and works as a new principle of nature, false affections are manifestly the result of "some extraordinary powerful influence of Satan and some great delusion."[6] Only a skilled minister could safely guide individuals to identify what is true and false in their own heart and to discern the wiles of Satan and the work of the Spirit. Edwards clearly was such and sought to open the eyes of the self-deceived.

Not Signs

In a somewhat surprising strategic decision, Edwards devoted the entire second section in *Religious Affections* to "false signs" of true piety. He was at some pains to say that these false signs "are no signs one way or the other." They do not necessarily negate the possibility that someone is saved, but on the other hand, these signs do not in themselves provide a strong argument that someone is in fact converted. Rather, these signs are simply chaff that tell little about the kernel or the reality of spiritual renewal in the heart and life.[7]

---

[5]Ibid., 2:209–10.
[6]Ibid. Twice in two paragraphs, Edwards identifies Satan as the main influence in false affections. Importantly, in 1744 James Davenport offered an apology for his behavior in citing "a false spirit" as the root cause. See Kidd, *Great Awakening*, 164.
[7]*Religious Affections*, WJE, 2:127.

Extraordinary Affections

One such false or inconclusive sign is that someone's affections
are raised to a high pitch. Certainly there are times when someone
is under deep conviction of sin or has affecting views of the love
of God when their affections are extraordinary. But heightened
affections in them do not mean that these are holy or even religious
affections at all. In contemporary terms, we can think of people
who watch the World Series or the Super Bowl and find their
hearts' affections raised to a fever pitch; that doesn't mean those
affections are spiritual. In the political realm, citizens' affections
can be raised to great joy or to deep anger by a political harangue,
but that doesn't mean those are holy affections.

Likewise in the spiritual realm, we can think of religious services that we have attended or watched on television. The music
and preaching were deeply affecting—our emotions were moved
and we thought that we would do anything in that moment for
Christ. For some, such strong emotions might even have physical effects—"holy laughter," "being slain in the Spirit," or even
saying words that are unknown to us. But those affections do
not actually move the will to bring about significant change in
the life: there is not a new sense of the heart that produces new
practices in our lives. Our affections may be great and holy, but
they are not in themselves "holy affections," nor do they possess
the characteristics of true religion.[8]

Talk of One's Experiences

Another inconclusive sign of whether holy affections are present
in the life of the individual is the ability to speak fluently and
at length about one's spiritual experience. As Edwards noted,
"We have no where any rule [in Scripture], by which to judge
ourselves or others to be in a good estate, from any such affect:

---

[8]Edwards addressed the issue of physical exercise in ibid., 2:132–35. It is important
to say that just as physical effects are not proofs of holy affections, they are not proofs
against them either. Edwards believed that his wife, Sarah, experienced just such physical
effects in 1742. See George M. Marsden, *Jonathan Edwards: A Life* (New Haven, CT:
Yale University Press, 2003), 240–49.

for this is but the religion of the mouth and of the tongue." A person may be "overfull of talk of his own experiences," which is a "dark sign." In fact, those with deceitful affections are much more prone to talk about them because they are motivated by spiritual pride and ambition, by a desire to be seen and known. This is an evidence that they are self-deceived and in a desperate spiritual condition.[9]

A Spirit Not Tested

A third inconclusive sign is that the individual cannot account for his spiritual awakening. Edwards does not discount that such a person might have experienced something spiritual—the effects of actions by a spirit not his or her own; but "it does not thence follow, that it was from the Spirit of God." What we must do, Edwards exhorted, is follow the instruction of 1 John 4:1, "Test the spirits to see whether they are from God." The problem is that the Devil presents himself as an angel of light; he has the ability to influence people in ways that seem "spiritual" but are not.[10]

Such individuals might be able to quote Scripture and might have biblical verses come directly to the mind, seemingly without conscious effort. Some people look at this as clear evidence that one is saved, but Edwards noted that the Bible itself provides no examples or rule to this effect. Rather, such people fail to recognize that "affections may arise on *occasion* of the Scripture, and not *properly come from* the Scripture, as the genuine fruit of the Scripture and by a right use of it; but from an abuse of it." The Devil himself can bring texts of Scripture to the mind and misapply them in such a way to draw people away from God rather than to him. After all, he tried to do just that in his temptation of Jesus, misquoting Psalm 91 in an effort to turn Christ himself away from his Father.[11]

---

[9]*Religious Affections*, WJE, 2:136, 137; see also p. 252.
[10]Ibid., 2:141–42. Edwards used 1 John 4:1 as his text for his sermon at Yale University, "Distinguishing Marks."
[11]*Religious Affections*, WJE, 2:143, 144. See also pp. 219–21.

An Initial Response to the Word

Along this same line, people might actually receive God's Word joyfully for a time, only to turn away from it in the end. Matthew 13 teaches Christians that "the stony-ground hearers had great joy from the Word" but in time of trial it is discovered that "there was no saving religion in these affections." That means there may be many in our congregations who hear God's Word gladly and give the appearance of growth, only to demonstrate in a time of trial in their marriage or family or work that there is no new sense of the heart and no genuine holy affections. Even if there is an appearance of great and passionate love to God and neighbor in these, their love will not continue because they have no grace in their hearts.[12]

Someone might even experience a sense of deliverance from sin or Satan and yet not truly be converted. Edwards supposed a situation where someone has experienced soul concern about their liability to eternal judgment and is feeling deep despair. Then, immediately and seemingly miraculously, he "is all at once delivered, by being firmly made to believe, through some delusion of Satan that God has pardoned him, and accepts him as the object of dear love, and promises him eternal life." This might happen through a dream or vision, perhaps "of a person with a beautiful countenance, smiling on him, and with arms open, and with blood dropping down, which the person conceives to be Christ." And yet, even with such an experience, it does not mean that the individual is truly saved or has experienced holy affections.[13]

Engagement in Worship

Finally, simply because individuals know freedom and engagement in worship does not mean that they have holy affections. Going to worship services, regular attendance in religious education, attending revival meetings—none of these means that someone

---

[12]Ibid., 2:145.
[13]Ibid., 2:149.

has truly been converted. In addition, a freedom in praising God or in singing and magnifying his name does not provide evidence of a change of life. Obviously, those who have experienced God's transforming grace long to be in God's presence, but that is not a sure sign of conversion.

All of these signs are really "not signs" of a changed life. They are inconclusive tests whether someone has truly experienced a new sense of the heart, new and holy affections that produce spiritual understanding and holy practice. Those who rest on these signs have the potential of being self-deceived about their condition. And that is because these signs can be counterfeited, produce hypocrisy, or subject the individual to "enthusiasm" in ways that cause him or her to be lost in the end.

Counterfeits

One reason that people often are self-deceived is that they have experienced counterfeit affections. Particularly, people mistake self-love for love for God; that is to say, they love God in an interested, as opposed to a disinterested, fashion. They love God for what they can get from him—joy, eternal life, deliverance from hell—rather than loving God for his own sake. They love God for what they think he is as opposed to what he actually is. And so, they think that they love God because he is a God of love and mercy, but not a God of judgment. "Men on such grounds as these," Edwards declares, "may love a God of their own forming in their imaginations, when they are far from loving such a God as reigns in heaven." Such love is actually a counterfeit and can inure people from genuine love for God.[14]

Edwards notes that not only can love to God and others be counterfeited, but all other sorts of affections can as well. These include sorrow for sin, fear of God, gracious gratitude, spiritual joy, earnest religious desires, and even a strong hope of eternal life. Those who are self-deceived experience joy, but they rejoice ultimately in themselves, not in God for God's own sake. They

---

[14]Ibid., 2:244.

might experience sorrow for sin, but it is counterfeit—it is worldly sorrow that leads to death, not godly sorrow that produces genuine repentance.[15]

Moreover, some may experience conviction and comfort in such a way that they believe they have been converted. And yet, the conviction might be counterfeited. Genuine conviction "consists in conviction of sinfulness of heart and practice, and of the dreadfulness of sin, as committed against a God of terrible majesty, infinite holiness and hatred of sin, and strict justice in punishing it." Counterfeit conviction is simply terror: frightful apprehensions of hell, a fiery pit, horrid devils, burning flames—none of these have to do with genuine conviction about the sinfulness of one's heart and life. This kind of conviction can come from the Devil himself and steer men into self-deception about their real problem.[16]

In a similar fashion, counterfeit comfort can actually distract sinners from seeking genuine gospel comfort. Those who experience counterfeit comfort often testify that "some comfortable sweet promise comes suddenly and wonderfully to their minds; and the manner of its coming makes 'em conclude it comes from God to them." From this extraordinary communication, people center their hopes for eternal salvation and continue in their lives self-deceived.[17]

The Devil can also deceive people about all those operations that look spiritual and seem to lead to God's grace, but do not. He can bring about false humiliations, false submissions, false comforts in an individual. The individual may feel humbled for his sins, may seem to submit to God, and even may appear to know divine comfort and yet remain an enemy to God. Satan can also counterfeit the order in which spiritual feelings occur—seeming conviction then comfort, terror then apparent submission, confession, and penitence. And so, people can be self-deceived about

[15]Ibid., 2:148, 249, 251.
[16]Ibid., 2:156.
[17]Ibid., 2:221.

their experience if they rest in their feelings or the order in which they have spiritual experiences.

Not only does the Devil deceive people, but even God's Spirit can operate in a common or ordinary fashion upon the hearts of men and women. The Holy Spirit does exercise upon the minds and hearts of "natural men," but "only moves, impresses, assists, improves, or some way acts upon natural principles." When this happens, God's Spirit "assists natural principles to do the same work to a greater degree, which they do of themselves by nature." For example, God's Spirit might assist lost people to do their work in such a way that it brings God's glory, even though that is not their intention. Lost men's reason might be assisted by God's Spirit to think and discover things, even when they fail to recognize God at work. None of this is saving, and yet, unconverted people might mistake these ordinary, common operations of God's Spirit as signs of God's favor and evidence of a good, eternal state.[18]

Hypocrisy

Another reason people can remain self-deceived is that they have been lulled into hypocrisy. "When once a hypocrite is thus established in a false hope," Edwards observed, "he han't those things to cause him to call his hope in question, that oftentimes are the occasion of the doubting of true saints." Hypocrites do not experience that cautious spirit which produces a continued striving after God in the life of the saint. In addition, they also do not have a deep knowledge about their own spiritual blindness and the deceitfulness of their own heart. While saints recognize their hearts are "deceitful above all else," the hypocrite rests on false comforts, fails to be self-reflective, and so falls prey to self-deception. Finally, hypocrites are not attacked by the Devil. While true Christians know the attacks of Satan as their great Enemy, hypocrites are not hounded by the Devil because it is in his interest for them to cherish false hopes.[19]

---

[18]Ibid., 2:206, 207.
[19]Ibid., 2:172.

Following the seventeenth-century American Puritan, Thomas Shepard, Edwards distinguished between "legal hypocrites" and "evangelical hypocrites." Legal hypocrites are those who "are deceived with their outward morality and external religion." Evangelical hypocrites are "those that are deceived with false discoveries and elevations; which often cry down works, and men's own righteousness and talk much of free grace." Of the two, Edwards clearly saw the latter as more dangerous. Evangelical hypocrites are self-deceived, having based their confidence of eternal salvation on false signs, and yet defending themselves by claiming that they have "the witness of the Spirit" (from Rom. 8:16–17). But not only are these people deceived—they are also stubborn. "They will maintain it against all manner of reason and evidence." Even though they are comfortable with their sin, still they doggedly maintain that they are saved, "which is a sure evidence of their delusion."[20]

In fact, hypocrites have little interest in holiness and see little beauty in it. Edwards noted,

> Such a difference is there between true saints, and natural men: natural men have no sense of the goodness and excellency of holy things; at least for their holiness; they have no taste of that kind of good; and so may be said not to know that divine good, or not to see it; it is wholly hid from them.

They are entirely blind to the beauty of God's holiness; they can't see or taste that it is good; they "have nothing of that spiritual taste which relishes this divine sweetness."[21]

Even though these hypocrites might persuade those who are truly godly that they are holy as well, that only increases their presumption. The fact is that believers "have not such a spirit of discerning, that they can certainly determine who are godly, and who are not. For though they know experimentally what true religion is, in the internal exercises of it; yet these are what

---

[20]Ibid., 2:173, 174.
[21]Ibid., 2:262, 263.

they can neither feel, nor see, in the heart of another." Because believers can only see another's external practice, they are easily deceived by the behavior of hypocrites. And hypocrites, in turn, allow the good opinion of others to reinforce their presumption about their eternal state.[22]

Of course, the great problem is that hypocrites have counterfeit affections, false convictions, and weightless comforts. As Edwards exclaimed, "How great therefore may the resemblance be, as to all outward expressions and appearances, between an hypocrite and a true saint!" Such counterfeits can fool even the most experienced pastor or theologian. And for those who presume to be able to discern who is saved and who is not, Edwards had little patience. "Those who have gone furthest this way, that have been most highly conceited of their faculty of discerning, and have appeared most forward, peremptorily and suddenly to determine the state of men's souls, have been hypocrites, who have known nothing of true religion." The separation of the sheep from the goats is a task that ultimately belongs to Jesus himself, and that awaits the end of the age.[23]

In short, Edwards did not hold out much hope for hypocrites. They "have been deceived with great false discoveries and affections, and are once settled in a false confidence, and a high conceit of their own supposed great experiences and privileges," he wrote.

> Such hypocrites are so conceited of their own wisdom, and so blinded and hardened with a very great self-righteousness (but very subtle and secret, under the disguise of great humility), and so invincible a fondness of their pleasing conceit, of their great exaltation, that it usually signifies nothing at all, to lay before them the most convincing evidences of their hypocrisy.

Next to those who have committed the unpardonable sin, hypocrites are in the most hopeless state.[24]

---

[22]Ibid., 2:181.
[23]Ibid., 2:182, 183, 185.
[24]Ibid., 2:196.

Enthusiasm

Another spiritual malady that produces self-deception is what the eighteenth century called "enthusiasm," a word that equated to "fanaticism." The "enthusiastical" were those who were becoming spiritually unhinged. As James Davenport demonstrated, this was an ever-present danger in the awakening. Edwards had to walk the razor's edge, affirming "great and high affections" on the one side while denouncing "enthusiasm" on the other.

The way he did this was to show how enthusiasm is another species of self-deception. For people to "expect to receive the saving influences of the Spirit of God, while they neglect a diligent improvement of the appointed means of grace, is unreasonable presumption," Edwards argued. "And to expect that the Spirit of God will savingly operate on their minds, without the Spirit's making use of means, as subservient to the effect, is enthusiastical."[25]

Likewise, those who emphasize a supernatural "leading of the Spirit" are in danger of enthusiasm. The way some talk about the Spirit's leading, it involves "giving them new precepts, by immediate inward speech or suggestion; and has in it no tasting the true excellency of things, or judging or discerning the nature of things at all." Such is not "spiritual understanding" but rather a form of "enthusiasm" in the same class as "imaginary sights of God and Christ and heaven, all supposed witnessing of the spirit, and testimonies of the love of God by immediate inward suggestion." These "enthusiastical impressions and applications of words of Scripture" simply are "impressions in the head" and imagination. Such a longing for immediate revelation and spiritual raptures puts one in the same class "as the Anabaptists in Germany, and many other raving enthusiasts like them." Clearly, that is not a good position to be in.[26]

The Real Problem

The real problem in all of this self-deception boils down to one issue: unbelief. Those who are hypocrites, who embrace counter-

[25]Ibid., 2:138.
[26]Ibid., 2:285, 286, 142.

feits, or who run off into enthusiasm are all unwilling to forsake their sin and turn to Christ in humble faith. Rather than seeking assurance in the way that God's Word teaches—"by mortifying corruption, and increasing in grace, and obtaining the lively exercises of it"—they seek out other pathways. If someone has the Spirit of the living God infused in his heart as a new principle of action, he will begin to put sin to death, put on new practices of holiness, and evidence this in new ways of living.[27]

And yet, pastorally speaking, dealing with people who are self-deceived is always difficult. When they are convinced that they have genuine grounds for a solid assurance of acceptance with God, pastors may find, like Edwards, those are difficult "wrong notions and ways in religion" to "beat them out of." In the end, the only hope for the self-deceived is God's grace: that the divine and supernatural light might shine into their hearts and lives to show them their sin—but more, to show them the real glory of Jesus.[28]

---

[27]Ibid., 2:195.
[28]Jonathan Edwards to Thomas Gillespie, July 1, 1751, *WJE*, 4:564.

CHAPTER 8

A Love Life

How the Affections Produce Genuine Virtue

One of Edwards's greatest essays was not published during his lifetime. He completed *The Nature of True Virtue*, along with its companion piece, *The End for Which God Created the World*, sometime in 1757. His literary executors found them in finished shape and published them in 1765. Philosophers and historians have long focused on Edwards's treatment of virtue as a significant accounting of the difference regeneration makes for public life as well as an attempt to spell out how the unregenerate can still work together for a just society. As important as the essay was for later reflection, it was to prove significant for Edwards's disciples. Ministers Joseph Bellamy and Samuel Hopkins, along with later Edwardsians, used *The Nature of True Virtue* to forge a powerful theological basis for social reform in the nineteenth century.[1]

Edwards had neither result in view when he wrote the piece. Rather, his focus was on "challenging the presumptions of the age," to use historian George Marsden's phrase. And especially, Edwards thought to knock out the foundations of modern thought with a swift right-left combination. As he told his friend and literary partner, Thomas Foxcroft:

> I have also written two other discourses, one on *God's End in Creating the World*; the other concerning *The Nature of True Virtue*. As it appeared to me, the modern opinions which prevail concerning these two things, stand very much as foundations of that fashionable scheme of divinity, which seems to have become almost universal.

His targets were some of the most important contemporary philosophers.

> My discourse on virtue is principally designed against that notion of virtue maintained by My Lord Shaftesbury, [Francis] Hutcheson, and [George] Turnbull; which seems to be most in vogue at this day, so far as I can perceive; which notion is calculated to show that all mankind are naturally disposed to virtue, and are without any native depravity.[2]

In other words, Edwards recognized global challenges that could shake the very foundations of biblical Christianity if they

---

[1]For the significance of *The Nature of True Virtue*, see Perry Miller, *Jonathan Edwards* (1949; repr., Amherst: University of Massachusetts Press, 1981), 284–305, and William K. Frankena, "Foreword," in Jonathan Edwards, *The Nature of True Virtue* (Ann Arbor: University of Michigan Press, 1960). For the use of this essay by his followers, see Mark Valeri, *Law and Providence in Joseph Bellamy's New England* (New York: Oxford University Press, 1994), and Joseph Conforti, *Samuel Hopkins and the New Divinity Movement: Calvinism, the Congregational Ministry, and the Great Awakenings* (Grand Rapids: Christian University Press, 1981).

[2]George M. Marsden, "Challenging the Presumptions of the Age: The Two Dissertations," in *The Legacy of Jonathan Edwards: American Religion and the Evangelical Tradition*, ed. D. G. Hart, Sean Michael Lucas, and Stephen J. Nichols (Grand Rapids: Baker, 2003), 99–113; Jonathan Edwards to Thomas Foxcroft, February 11, 1757, in *The Works of Jonathan Edwards* (hereafter *WJE*), vol. 16, *Letters and Personal Writings*, ed. George S. Claghorn (New Haven, CT: Yale University Press, 1998), 696.

went unanswered. While scholars have lumped these challenges under the heading of "Enlightenment religion," it is possible to see four major prongs in the challenge provided by the Enlightenment. First was a challenge to the nature of biblical revelation. Enlightenment religionists, whom we know as deists, simply ruled the idea of the supernatural out of court as irrational. Hence, biblical testimony to miracles and prophecy is untrue and impossible; such miracles involve all sorts of scientific absurdities and historical contradictions. The chief biblical absurdity, representing the second challenge, is Trinitarianism. It was clear to modern reason that the idea of one God in three persons is a mathematical impossibility. Hence, God is one, whom Jesus called Father, and Jesus was a moral being who became the Son of God through what he suffered. A third challenge that Enlightenment religion offered centered on the nature of religious experience. Human beings are not inherently sinful, but good; all have a basic moral sense that guides them in the world and provides the basis for society. Because humans are good, they do not need a Redeemer who died in their place; the idea of Christ's blood of substitutionary sacrifice is repulsive to deists. Humans do not need supernatural conversion or a divine-human Savior, but instruction in ethical behavior. A final challenge was how to account for a virtuous society. Following from their understanding of human nature, Enlightenment thinkers sought to build a society on the common moral sense that pervades humankind. Rather than appealing to biblical revelation, deist intellectuals appealed to nature, nature's laws, and self-evident truths within and outside human beings in order to ground moral action and societal structure.[3]

In sum, at the heart of deist or Enlightenment religion was the idea that "religion is morality." Or to put it differently, the only true religion is one that affirms human beings and their natural

---

[3]This paragraph summarizes a great deal of literature. Among the first places to consult would be Gerald R. McDermott, *Jonathan Edwards Confronts the Gods: Christian Theology, Enlightenment Religion, and Non-Christian Faiths* (New York: Oxford University Press, 2000), and Avihu Zakai, *Jonathan Edwards's Philosophy of History: The Reenchantment of the World in the Age of Enlightenment* (Princeton, NJ: Princeton University Press, 2003).

capacities along with a general affirmation of God's existence and beneficent control over the world. Only such a view of things accords with reason and the moral sense belonging to each human being. Humans' focus should be on forging a world that is moral and ethical, centered on five basic truths: the existence of God, the rational worship of God, the need for an ethical response to that worship, the need for moral improvement ("repentance"), and the promise of reward and punishment in the afterlife.[4]

Much of Edwards's writing can be viewed as a response to the global challenge that Enlightenment religion represented. In particular, his apologetic centered on the rationality of Trinitarian faith, the reality of human depravity and the bondage of the human will, the solid basis that religious experience provides for faith in this world, the trustworthy character of biblical revelation as history, and a rational account of moral virtue that aligns with biblical revelation. But Edwards sought to meet this global challenge because he was worried about the local effects in his congregation and colony. As historian Gerald McDermott notes, "Edwards's struggle with Arminianism was but a battle in a life-long war with deism." Read in this light, Edwards's declaration in his 1737 *Faithful Narrative* that "about this time, began the great noise that was in this part of country about Arminianism, which seemed to appear with a very threatening aspect upon the interest of religion" takes on a different cast. Far from a concern about "free will" evangelicals (such as latter-day Wesleyan Methodists or Free Will Baptists), Edwards's concern about Arminianism was actually a concern about the "Deist challenge" coming to the very banks of the Connecticut River.[5]

True Virtue

Therefore, *The Nature of True Virtue* was actually a response to global challenges that were becoming local, challenges that

[4]McDermott, *Jonathan Edwards Confronts the Gods*, 21; E. Brooks Holifield, *Theology in America: Christian Thought from the Age of the Puritans to the Civil War* (New Haven, CT: Yale University Press, 2003), 159–72.
[5]McDermott, *Jonathan Edwards Confronts the Gods*, 47; Jonathan Edwards, "Faithful Narrative of the Surprising Work of God," in *WJE*, vol. 4, *The Great Awakening*, ed. C. C. Goen (New Haven, CT: Yale University Press, 1972), 148.

could undo biblical Christianity in the godly commonwealth. Since the entire question of the nature of true virtue was at the heart of these challenges that Edwards faced, how did he define "true virtue"? Early in his essay he observed that "true virtue most essentially consists in benevolence to Being in general." But this definition provokes as many questions as it answers. Notice that Edwards claimed that true virtue in its essence consists in love—in particular, "benevolence." That is an important word. By benevolence, he meant love "as it respects the good enjoyed or to be enjoyed *by* the beloved." This is distinguished from love as complacence, a love "as it respects good to be enjoyed *in* the beloved." Thus benevolence is "that disposition which a man has who desires or delights in the good of another." It is, above all other considerations, "the main thing in Christian love, the most essential thing."[6]

But what is the object of this benevolence? "Being in general," Edwards taught. What is that? For the answer, once again it is necessary to pay attention to Edwards's early reflections on "excellency," written in his early twenties. Toward the end of his entry in his notebook on "The Mind," he wrote, "This is an universal definition of excellency: the consent of being to being, or being's consent to entity. The more the consent is, and the more extensive, the greater is the excellency." By "entity," Edwards meant "being in general," the ground of being for all other beings that derive existence from that ground. And who is that? It is God himself. And so, what is excellency? It is the delightful and pleasurable consent of being to God himself, who is the ground of all existence.[7]

Edwards applied this approach to his essay on true virtue. There, he defines "Being in general" as "the great system of universal existence." This system of existence is limited to intelligent existence, and "not inanimate things, or beings that have

---

[6]Jonathan Edwards, "The Nature of True Virtue," in *WJE*, vol. 8, *Ethical Writings*, ed. Paul Ramsey (New Haven, CT: Yale University Press, 1989), 540; Jonathan Edwards, "Charity and Its Fruits," in *WJE*, 8:212–13, emphasis original.
[7]Jonathan Edwards, "The Mind," in *WJE*, vol. 6, *Scientific and Philosophical Writings*, ed. Wallace E. Anderson (New Haven, CT: Yale University Press, 1980), 336 (no. 1).

no perception or will, which are not properly capable objects of benevolence." And God is that being who has the most existence, "that Being who has most of being, or has the greatest share of existence"; hence, God himself is the first great object of benevolent love. Indeed, Edwards goes so far as to say, "'Tis evident that true virtue must chiefly consist in love to God; the Being of beings, infinitely the greatest and best of beings."[8]

The second object of benevolence is that universe of animate creation that partakes of "Being in general." In loving this secondary object of pure benevolence, God does not create two distinct and separate loves, one to God and one to humans. Rather, for Edwards, love is all of the same piece of cloth; or better, love to God and to humans springs from the same disposition of heart. And yet, if it were possible to have benevolent love for humankind, so much so that it extended to all the world of humanity, and not have love for God, then that love would not be truly virtuous love. It would be a type of love that is secondary and analogous to truly virtuous love, but not true virtue.[9]

Thus, Edwards was saying that true virtue in its essence consists in disinterested love to God himself and then, secondarily, to human beings. And it is modeled upon and is in response to God's love for himself. The triune God is himself the most excellent being because he most perfectly "consents" to himself, most unreservedly and disinterestedly delights in himself. As already noted, God's own being consists in God's love for himself. And as God the Spirit is the holy delight and love that God has for himself, so he has infused himself into the hearts of his people. When the Scriptures speak of the indwelling Spirit, "it will signify much the same thing if it be said, a divine temper or disposition dwells in us or fills us. Now the temper or disposition or affection of God is no other than infinite love." And thus, when the Holy Spirit indwells the individual, it is as much as saying a new disposition of love is infused in the individual, so that, whereas the individual could not love before, now God loves through the individual—and yet not in such a way as

---

[8] "Nature of True Virtue," *WJE*, 8:541, 542, 545–46, 550.
[9] Ibid., 8:603.

to assimilate the individual's personality. The Spirit is infused and dwells in the soul "as an holy principle and divine nature." This divine nature's essence is found in love. Thus, the individual who exercises benevolent love does so motivated by the infused nature of God, by the disposition of love or—what is the same thing—by the Spirit of God. And so it is possible for a human being to desire and delight in the good of another, in the delight and enjoyment that the other has, and to do so in a disinterested fashion.[10]

Fruits of Benevolence

What does a life look like that is characterized by desiring and delighting in God for God's own sake and in others for their own sake? What is the fruit of disinterested benevolence?

Holiness

One fruit of benevolence is holiness. This is true generally because all genuine Christian graces incline the individual to holiness. But love is the chief of the graces. Not surprisingly, Edwards noted, "Charity is opposite to all unrighteousness, or evil doings or practice, and it tends to all holy practice." How will this tendency to holiness be expressed in practice? This benevolent love to being in general disposes men to actions that are contrary to fallen human nature and that satisfy the demands of the moral law. And that is because at the heart of God's law is love—those who live holy lives in conformity to God's law love others.[11]

For example, this type of benevolent love disposes individuals to bear patiently with evil acts committed against them. If individuals had benevolence that disposed them to endure evil, such would prevent contention and strife

in our towns and public societies in the management of all our public affairs. . . . Our affairs would all be carried on without any fierceness, without rage and bitterness of spirit, without

---

[10]Jonathan Edwards, "The 'Miscellanies,' no. 396," in *WJE*, vol. 13, *The "Miscellanies," a–500*, ed. Thomas A. Schafer (New Haven, CT: Yale University Press, 1994), 462; "Charity and Its Fruits," *WJE*, 8:158, 332.

[11]"Charity and Its Fruits," *WJE*, 8:294.

harsh and opprobrious expressions to others, and malignant
backbiting and contemptuous speeches behind others' backs.

Rather than having a "bitter, exasperated countenance," those
who exercise love to God and humans have words and behavior
that "savor of peaceableness and calmness," intending to seek
the other's good and not his harm.[12]

Love disposes individuals to be kind to others in the face
of evil. Such individuals seek to reclaim "the souls of vicious
persons" by doing good to them in a variety of ways: by coun-
seling, warnings, and instructing; by providing a good example;
or by outward kindnesses, such as extending financial support.
And even when there is no opportunity to do good, if we are
animated by holy love, we will be "willing to suffer considerably
in our own interest for the sake of peace rather than do what
we have opportunity to do to defend ourselves." Such kindness
demonstrates both consent to the divine will and a delight in others that is willing to sacrifice self rather than cause contention.[13]

Absolute benevolence disposes us not to begrudge other
people's prosperity, but rather disposes us to humility. Benevolence eliminates attitudes toward others that would seek to bring
superiors down to a lower level. Likewise, a true disposition of
love drives men to prevent in themselves aspiring, ambitious,
or ostentatious behavior. No longer are individuals inflexible in
standing upon their own opinions, but rather ready to yield to
others as superior and ready to be taught.[14]

Furthermore, love disposes men not to be selfish, concerned
only with their private affairs; rather, it drives them to become
involved in civic affairs. Indeed, Edwards wrote, "A man of a
right spirit is not of a narrow, private spirit; but he is greatly concerned for the good of the public community to which he belongs,
and particularly of the town where he dwells." As one who has

---

[12]Ibid., 8:204, 188.
[13]Ibid., 8:211, 191.
[14]Ibid., 8:208, 238–42.

God's own disposition indwelling him, such a man willingly and disinterestedly seeks the benefit of the entire community.[15]

Finally, love disposes individuals to act toward others in a way that is not bitter or censorious. Love disposes men to be angry in a righteous way, not because men sin against their persons, but rather because when men sin, they do so against God. As Edwards observed, "An envious Christian, a malicious Christian, a cold and hard-hearted Christian is the greatest absurdity and contradiction. It is as if one should speak of dark brightness or of a false truth." Those who have a new disposition who is the Spirit of God himself indwelling them should bear God's own character of love toward enemies and holy patience. These concrete, holy actions demonstrate genuine virtue motivated by general, disinterested benevolence.[16]

Community

Second, another fruit of benevolence is genuine community. Because true virtue is benevolence to being in general, there is a fundamental consent to God and his ways. Even more, there is a union with God, his desires and designs, and a reflection of his character. In this way, the regenerate form a union with being in general.

> In pure love to others (i.e. love not arising from self-love) there's a union of the heart with others; a kind of enlargement of the mind, whereby it extends itself as to take others into a man's self: and therefore it implies a disposition to feel, to desire, and to act as though others were one with ourselves.

This union with others is what Edwards meant by community; benevolence has a tendency to community. And for Edwards, the great reality and illustration of this tendency of benevolence will be realized in heaven.[17]

---

[15]Ibid., 8:260.
[16]Ibid., 8:278, 147.
[17]"Nature of True Virtue," *WJE*, 8:589.

One of Edwards's greatest sermons is "Heaven Is a World of Love," which was the final sermon in his series "Charity and Its Fruits." In the sermon, Edwards identified the great archetype of benevolence to being in general and this tendency to community in heaven. The communion of the truly virtuous on earth is merely a shadow that corresponds to the heavenly reality.

> What rest is there in that world which the God of love and peace fills with his glorious presence, where the Lamb of God lives and reigns, and fills that world with the pleasant beams of his love; where is nothing to give any offense, no object to be seen but what has perfect sweetness and amiableness; where the saints shall find and enjoy all which they love, and so be perfectly satisfied; where there is no enemy and no enmity in any heart, but perfect love in all to everyone; where there is a perfect harmony between the higher and the lower ranks of inhabitants of that world, none envying another, but everyone resting and rejoicing in the happiness of every other. All their love is holy, humble, and perfectly Christian, without the least impurity or carnality; where love is always mutual, where the love of the beloved is answerable to the love of the lovers; where there is no hypocrisy or dissembling, but perfect simplicity and sincerity; where there is no treachery, unfaithfulness or inconstancy, nor any such thing as jealousy. . . . And all this in a garden of love, the Paradise of God, where everything has the cast of holy love, and everything conspires to promote and stir up love, and nothing to interrupt its exercises.[18]

Here is the summation of all that Edwards desired in this ethic of benevolence to being in general: these two great tendencies of holiness and community side-by-side in glorious display. In heaven, where there will be no sin and no inordinate self-love to interrupt this love for general existence and for God, true community exists—no envy, no coveting, no censoriousness, no anger. Rather, there will be true sincerity, purity, and fervency in the

---

[18]"Charity and Its Fruits," *WJE*, 8:384–85. For further discussion of Edwards's teaching on heaven, see Amy Plantinga Pauw, "'Heaven Is a World of Love': Edwards on Heaven and the Trinity," *Calvin Theological Journal* 30 (1995): 392–401.

love for others and for God. And thus, holiness and community will be furthered. With heaven as the pattern, the Christian's duty and desire, in line with his new disposition and holy affections, is to see things done on earth as they are in heaven.

Secondary Virtue

Obviously, since this new disposition that enables us to love being in general is the Spirit himself, such virtue is not natural to humankind. Unregenerate human beings have a type of virtue that resembles true virtue, but it is not actually virtuous, because it is only love to a private sphere and for private interest.

In fact, the love that the unregenerate exercise for their private spheres and interests is actually a form of self-love. Edwards defined self-love as "a man's regard to his confined *private self*, or love to himself with respect to his *private interest.*" Self-love is not illegitimate. In fact, benevolence is not necessarily opposed to self-love; benevolence is one's interest to love being in general, to love God and others. Edwards argued that for a man to remain opposite his own happiness would be the same as destroying that person's being, for loving one's own happiness is as necessary to human nature as the faculty of will. Or again, he demonstrated that the "golden rule" is based in part on an understanding of what one's own happiness consists in. Neither of these examples of self-love is opposite to pure benevolence required in true virtue. In fact, all human beings, regenerate and unregenerate, live their lives motivated in some sense by self-love.[19]

The difference between the self-love of the regenerate and the unregenerate centers on "inordinate self-love." How does inordinate self-love manifest itself? Two ways. First, love for one's own happiness may be too great when compared with love for another's happiness. If this balance between self-love and love for others is unregulated and self-love reigns supreme, then this self-love is inordinate and thus an illegitimate principle.[20]

---

[19]"Nature of True Virtue," *WJE*, 8:577; "Charity and Its Fruits," *WJE*, 8:254–55.
[20]"Charity and Its Fruits," *WJE*, 8:256–57.

Second, love for one's own happiness may consist in "placing that happiness in things which are confined to himself." This selfishness may not be limited strictly to things that impact directly on one's own happiness. However, if love falls short of "being in general," and, particularly, if an individual's love falls short of true love for God, then it is inordinate self-love. The problem is that when one is motivated by love that is private, this "private affection" cannot help but to devolve into a party spirit, which "will set a person *against* general existence, and make him an enemy to it." One who stands in opposition to general existence, at least some part of it, cannot have a pure benevolence that tends to genuine community and is motivated for the common good. Hence, actions motivated by self-love fall short of true virtue.[21]

This self-love, which is exercised for its own party and therefore finds itself in dissent from being in general, causes the unregenerate person to experience a sense of dissonance within himself. Self-love has its own tendency to self-union; that is, "self-love implies an inclination to feel and act as one with ourselves." And yet, ironically, when a person acts as one with himself, such does not actually serve his own greatest happiness. Instead, his greatest happiness would be served by benevolence to being in general. The individual motivated by self-love feels "uneasy in a consciousness of being inconsistent with himself and, as it were, against himself in his own actions." This natural tendency, which exists in every human breast, to self-union, and which exercises itself when it experiences dissonance, Edwards called "natural conscience."[22]

This natural conscience consists in two things: self-consistency and a "sense of desert." Self-consistency is "that disposition to approve or to disapprove the moral treatment which passes between us and others, from a determination of the mind to be easy, or uneasy, in a consciousness of our being consistent or inconsistent with ourselves." The way one can determine whether he is self-consistent is by placing himself in the other party's

---

[21] Ibid.; "Nature of True Virtue," *WJE*, 8:555.
[22] "Nature of True Virtue," *WJE*, 8:589.

position. This is done habitually, and it provides the basis for determining whether one has acted in a way consistent with his own expectations.[23]

A "sense of desert" is a feeling that one has received what he has deserved, especially when that person places himself in the other's position. This substitution is the key to the way the conscience operates, and the standard that judges this substitution is self-love, or self-union. Notice, though, how justice and self-love operate. Edwards called this combination of justice (or desert) and self-love "that moral sense" which had been insisted on by the moral philosophers of the day. Natural conscience is the moral sense.[24]

Self-love, motivating the individual to practice that is consonant with self-union, produces actions that are analogous to true virtue, but not genuinely virtuous. Because these actions produced by self-love are analogous to and partake in something of the nature of true virtue, "they are beautiful within their own private sphere; that is, they appear beautiful if we confine our views to that private system." However, this is the reason why actions motivated and produced by self-love fail to be truly virtuous: because self-love is private in its very definition, actions motivated by it are private and personal, the very opposite of universal benevolence. If the private sphere of self-love were to include "being in general," then that individual's benevolence would be truly beautiful, "all things considered." However, every person's private sphere of self-love is "so far from containing the sum of universal Being, or comprehending all existence which we stand related to, that it contains but an infinitely small part of it." The blind spot in all private spheres or systems of self-love resides in the fact that "they are ready to leave the Divine Being out of their view." Any system of love that excludes God is flawed and cannot achieve true virtue. Such systems may produce natural beauty or secondary virtue, but they will fall short of true virtue.[25]

[23]Ibid., 8:589.
[24]Ibid., 8:589, 592.
[25]Ibid., 8:610.

Does this mean that natural beauty or secondary virtue is worthless in Edwards's estimation? Edwards believed that this secondary virtue produced by self-love is necessary for an ordering of society, particularly of a society where there is no hope of a completely regenerate populace. For example, the right ordering of conscience with its sense of justice, if viewed in a collective light, gives the basis for a just punishment of crimes against the state. Likewise, self-love, loving others in light of their own interest, will provide and care for others in such a manner as to produce secondary virtue. However, all of this falls far short of that true virtue that is required by God and will be demanded at the final accounting.[26]

Affections and Virtues

In many ways, Edwards's account of true virtue bears a striking resemblance to his account of holy affections. After all, if God communicates himself in such a way that disinterested, practical, holy love to God and others is the result, that looks like the new sense of the heart infused by the Spirit, which grants the redeemed a new disposition or habit, which in turn acts out in new practices of holiness. Edwards may have used more philosophical language, but his thought was consistent here: holy affections produce true virtue, and only those who know such affections can produce true virtue.

Edwards pulled the strands together toward the end of *The Nature of True Virtue*. He wrote, "These things may help us to understand why that spiritual and divine sense, by which those that are truly virtuous and holy perceive the excellency of true virtue, is in the sacred Scriptures called by the name of light, knowledge, understanding, etc." Here are all Edwards's key terms: *divine sense, excellency, perception, light, spiritual understanding.* In one place, he brought together his various themes. Only those who have the new sense, who know a divine and supernatural light, can live truly virtuous lives. Only these have perceived the

---

[26]Ibid., 8:612.

excellency, the beauty, of God's revelation and of God himself. Only these have genuine spiritual knowledge and understanding. Only these have love communicated from God himself to share with others and to reflect back to God. "The want of this spiritual sense, and the prevalence of those dispositions that are contrary to it, tends to darken and distract the mind, and dreadfully to delude and confound men's understandings," he concluded. Holy affections—there is no genuine virtue without them.[27]

---

[27]Ibid., 8:622, 623.

CHAPTER 9

Means of Grace

The Ministry of the Word

Even though Edwards taught about a "spiritual and divine light, immediately imparted to the soul by God," that did not mean that he denigrated the work of the "ordinary means of grace." Far from it. "A person can't have spiritual light without the Word." In a similar fashion, true religion consists in holy affections, and because this is the case,

> such means are to be desired, as have much of a tendency to move the affections. Such books, and such a way of preaching the Word, and administration of ordinances, and such a way of worshiping God in prayer, and singing praises, is much to be desired, as has a tendency to affect the hearts of those who attend these means.

Edwards's teaching on light and affections demands a right use of God's means of grace, especially the ministry of the Word, the administration of the sacraments, and prayer.[1]

But Edwards gave careful attention to the relationship between God's granting of grace immediately (or without mediation) and a person's right use of God's means of grace. In Edwards's private notebooks, "The 'Miscellanies,'" he wrestled with these matters. In one thorough statement, he observed,

> Grace is from God as immediately and directly as light is from the sun; and that notwithstanding the means that are improved, such as word, ordinances, etc. For though these are made use of, yet they have no influence to produce grace, either as causes or instruments, or any other way; and yet they are concerned in the affair of the production of grace, and are necessary in order to it.

How are the means of grace necessary?[2]

For one thing, the means of grace "supply the mind with notions, or speculative ideas, of the things of religion, and thus give an opportunity for grace to act upon, when God shall be pleased to infuse it." Even if there were a new principle of grace in the heart, "sensible knowledge," yet if there were not "speculative knowledge" already present, it could not act and bring about conversion, Edwards held. And so, it is our responsibility to fill our minds with true biblical and doctrinal commitments. "The more fully we are supplied with these notions, the greater opportunity has grace to act, and to act more suitably to the nature of things when God infuses it, because it has more objects to act upon, and one object illustrates another." Likewise, these commitments should be held in a "lively" and "vigorous" fashion because such indicates that our reason is assenting to the truth,

---

[1]Jonathan Edwards, "A Divine and Supernatural Light," in *The Works of Jonathan Edwards* (hereafter *WJE*), vol. 17, *Sermons and Discourses, 1730–1733*, ed. Mark Valeri (New Haven, CT: Yale University Press, 1999), 410; Jonathan Edwards, *WJE*, vol. 2, *Religious Affections*, ed. John E. Smith (New Haven, CT: Yale University Press, 1959), 121, 114–16.

[2]Jonathan Edwards, "The 'Miscellanies,' no. 539," in *WJE*, vol. 18, *The "Miscellanies," 501–832*, ed. Ava Chamberlain (New Haven, CT: Yale University Press, 2000), 84.

even before the Spirit is infused to move the affections and gain the movement of the will. As a result, the means of grace are important for the Christian life; they do not cause grace, but they are used by the Spirit to grant converting grace.[3]

Perhaps that is why Edwards argued that "'tis the excellency of a minister of the gospel to be both a burning and a shining light." Such was the propositional (or "doctrinal") statement of Jonathan Edwards's second published ordination sermon. Preached in August 1744 for Robert Abercrombie at his ordination and installation as the minister of the congregational church in Pelham, Massachusetts, this sermon served as a rich and important resource for understanding how Edwards thought about the ministry of the Word and its relationship to the Christian life.[4]

The first clue to the sermon's importance is the theme of "excellency," which had such an important place in Edwards's thought. For Edwards, excellency suggested proportion, harmony, equality, consent of the parts to the whole. As philosopher Wallace Anderson has noted, excellency served as both a moral and an aesthetic evaluation; and the great example of excellency, morally and aesthetically speaking, was Jesus Christ himself, who brought together seemingly opposite characteristics in perfect harmony and beauty. So, for a minister to be both morally and aesthetically excellent, he must exemplify in perfect harmony both characteristics of light, both a burning and a shining light. Or as Edwards himself put it, "When light and heat are thus united in a minister of the gospel, it shows that each is genuine, and of a right kind, and that both are divine. Divine light is attended with heat; and so, on the other hand, a truly divine and holy heat and ardor is ever accompanied with light." The task of ministry is to be both divine light and holy heat for the benefit of the souls of humankind.[5]

---

[3]Ibid., 18:85–87.

[4]Jonathan Edwards, "The True Excellency of a Minister of the Gospel," in *WJE*, vol. 25, *Sermons and Discourses, 1743–1758*, ed. Wilson H. Kimnach (New Haven, CT: Yale University Press, 2006), 87.

[5]Jonathan Edwards, "The Mind," in *WJE*, vol. 6, *Scientific and Philosophical Writings*, ed. Wallace E. Anderson (New Haven, CT: Yale University Press, 1980), 81, 332–38 (no. 1); Jonathan Edwards, "The Excellency of Jesus Christ," in *WJE*, vol. 19, *Sermons*

Such reflection on the ministry of the Word was far from unusual for Edwards. On the public occasions of ordinations, which gave opportunity for reflection on the ministerial task, he spent a great deal of time pondering his life's work and especially how the ministry of the Word serves "the precious and immortal souls of men committed to their care and trust by the Lord Jesus Christ." It is not surprising that Edwards, as a preacher of God's Word, believed that the most important means that God has granted to ministers for caring for these souls is the preaching ministry of God's Word.[6]

Edwards thought deeply and repeatedly about how the preaching of God's Word serves to reflect the light of Christ into the very hearts of parishioners.

> Ministers are set to be lights to the souls of men in this respect, as they are to be the means of imparting divine truth to them, and bringing into their view the most glorious and excellent objects, and of leading them to, and assisting them in the contemplation of those things that angels desire to look into.

In this way, God uses the ministry of his Word to impart a divine and supernatural light to the human heart, moving listeners' affections, transforming their actions, and shaping them to be more like Jesus. Simply put, the Christian life—or for Edwards, the development of truly holy affections—could not occur without a theologically thoughtful, genuinely pious, and biblically oriented ministry of the Word.[7]

The Minister's Calling

That Edwards had a high view of the minister's calling and task is not surprising. It was an inheritance of colonial New England's continued appreciation for pastoral ministry as a divine office

and Discourses, 1734–1738, ed. M. X. Lesser (New Haven, CT: Yale University Press, 2001), 563–94.
[6]Jonathan Edwards, "The Great Concern of a Watchman for Souls," in *WJE*, 25:63; Jonathan Edwards, "The Church's Marriage to Her Sons, and Her God," in *WJE*, 25:171.
[7]"True Excellency of a Minister of the Gospel," *WJE*, 25:90; "A Divine and Supernatural Light," *WJE*, 17:416–17.

and calling and not merely a profession. In addition, both his father and grandfather held extremely high views of ministerial calling and authority, regularly doing battle with their congregations by insisting on ministerial prerogatives and in ordering the weekly rhythms of community and congregational life. While these sources contributed to his understanding, Edwards's conception of the ministry was also shaped by his own exploration of biblical-theological metaphors.[8]

Ministers as Married to the Bride

One powerful complex of images to describe ministerial calling was marital. In an ordination sermon delivered for Samuel Buell in 1746, Edwards teased out the imagery of Isaiah 62:4–5 to suggest that the relationship between the minister and his congregation was modeled upon the marriage union that Christ had with his church. When one is ordained to ministry, he is "espoused" to the church in general—he bears a concern for the church of Christ in general, its interests and welfare, more than he would as a private person. The minister is espoused to a particular congregation, which Edwards likened to "a young man's marrying a virgin." In this union between minister and congregation, there is to be "mutual regard and affection"; both minister and congregation are to attribute the highest and purest motives to one another. Such a relationship should bring great joy, mutual sympathy and helpfulness to minister and people alike. As a husband cares for his wife, Edwards suggested, so a minister should care for his particular church.[9]

In this marital imagery, ministers serve a second role—that of proxy in the marriage between Christ and his bride, the church. "Ministers espouse the church entirely as Christ's ambassadors," Edwards noted, "as representing him and standing in his stead,

---

[8]For sources that explain this point in more detail, see Patricia J. Tracy, *Jonathan Edwards, Pastor: Religion and Society in Eighteenth-Century Northampton* (New York: Hill and Wang, 1978), 13–50, and Kenneth Pieter Minkema, "The Edwardses: A Ministerial Family in Eighteenth-Century New England" (PhD diss., University of Connecticut, 1988), esp. 15–147.

[9]"Church's Marriage to Her Sons," *WJE*, 25:172–73.

being sent forth by him to be married to her in his name, that by this means she may be married to him." The union between minister and people "is but a shadow" pointing toward the union that the Christian individually and corporately has with Jesus Christ. And so, in caring for his people, the minister offers not his own care, but the care of Jesus. "All that tender care which a faithful minister takes of his people as a kind of spiritual husband, to provide for them, to lead and feed them, and comfort them, is not as looking upon them [as] his own bride, but his master's." Everything a minister does for his people is on Christ's behalf, draws from Christ's own love for his bride, and points people to Christ as their true husband and lover.[10]

Ministers as Lights

Another set of metaphors that Edwards used to unpack the nature of ministerial calling was among his favorite: light. Ministers are granted God's Spirit in order to communicate "the golden oil or divine grace to God's people." In Edwards's day, this holy grace would enable God's people to be lights to a generation that desperately needed to know the source of all good. In fact, ministers are both a "shining light" and a "burning light" for God's people. To help ministers picture this, Edwards compared them to stars, noting that "the ministers of Christ are as it were the stars that encompass this glorious fountain of light, to receive and reflect his beams, and give light to the souls of men." He also used optics to picture the way ministers communicated the light of Christ.

> [Ministers] are called burning and shining lights but they have neither light nor heat any further than as they derive it from the sun of righteousness and can communicate no light nor life nor fruitfulness to their hearers any further than they are made use of as glasses to convey and reflect the beams of the light of the world.[11]

[10]Ibid., 25:170, 177, 184.
[11]Jonathan Edwards, "Sons of Oil, Heavenly Lights," in *WJE*, 25:263; "True Excellency of a Minister of the Gospel," *WJE*, 25:89; Jonathan Edwards, "Sermon on Matt.

As burning and shining lights, ministers shine in "to clear divine truths and to refute errors, and to reclaim and correct God's people wherein in any respect they have been mistaken and have been going out of the way of duty." And yet there is a continuing need to balance the burning and shining aspects of light. A minister who has light but no heat "entertains his auditory with learned discourses, without a savor of the power of godliness or any appearance of fervency of spirit and zeal for God and the good of souls." As a result, he may "gratify itching ears and fill the heads of people with empty notions; but will not be very likely to reach their hearts, or save their souls." On the other hand, a minister who has vehement, intemperate, and zealous heat "will be likely to kindle the like unhallowed flame in his people, and to fire their corrupt passions and affections; but will never make them better, nor lead them a step toward heaven." If ministers would stir up holy affections in the hearts of their people, they must be shining *and* burning lights.[12]

Ministers as Servants

A third image that Edwards used to describe ministers was "servants." As he put it in a sermon on John 13:15–16, "The work and business of ministers of the gospel is as it were that of servants, to wash and cleanse the souls of men." He meant that ministers must be characterized by the "same spirit of humility and lowliness of heart. . . . the same spirit of heavenly-mindedness and contempt of the glory, wealth and pleasures of this world . . . the same spirit of devotion and fervent love to God" that characterized Jesus himself. Edwards also compared ministers to farmers or "husbandmen," pointing out that "ministers of the Gospel are the servants of the owner of the field that are sent forth to sow his seed." To be a servant or a husbandman is strenuous work. "Ministers are not called to be idle, but to

---

13:3–4(a)," in *WJE Online*, vol. 56, *Sermons, Series II, July–December 1740* (Jonathan Edwards Center at Yale University, 2008).
[12]Jonathan Edwards, "One Great End in God's Appointing the Gospel Ministry," in *WJE*, 25:444; "True Excellency of a Minister of the Gospel," *WJE*, 25:96.

labor . . . the business of a faithful minister tis a business of great and continual labor."[13]

Because the ministry requires "hard labor," "constant care, or continual oversight," Edwards called for continued personal formation and spiritual discipline. He laid it down as a basic axiom that "the ministers of Christ ought to be eminently gracious and near to Christ." This means that ministers "should have their entire and continual dependence on Christ for all fitness for their work and assistance and success in it." Abiding and resting in Christ by faith, clinging to his promises, studying his Word, continuing in "secret converse with him," depending on him to bear fruit—all are requirements for pastoral leaders because "they have no light of their own but all is derived from Christ, who is the light of the world, and they can be of no use to enlighten the souls of men unless held up by Christ."[14]

These disciplines are possible only because ministers experience genuine grace from God in Christ by the Spirit. Faithful ministers have experienced true grace, which has "an exceeding energy in it. And the reason is, that God is in it; it is a divine principle, a participation of the divine nature, and a communication of divine life, of the life of a risen Savior, who exerts himself in the hearts of the saints." This genuine grace produces genuine piety, which is "nothing remaining only in the head, or consisting in any speculative knowledge or opinions, or outward morality or forms of religion; it reaches the heart, is chiefly seated there, and burns there. There is a holy ardor in everything that belongs to true grace." Having the Spirit of Christ indwelling, the minister's heart "burns with love to Christ, and fervent desires of the advancement of his kingdom and glory; and also with ardent love to the souls of men, and desires for their salvation."[15]

---

[13]Jonathan Edwards, "Christ the Great Example of Gospel Ministers," in *WJE*, 25:335, 336; "Sermon on Matt. 13:3–4(a)."

[14]"Sons of Oil, Heavenly Lights," *WJE*, 25:264, 265, 266; "Christ the Great Example of Gospel Ministers," *WJE*, 25:346; "Sermon on Matt. 13:3–4(a)."

[15]"True Excellency of a Minister of the Gospel," *WJE*, 25:91, 92.

As a faithful minister grasps the basic metaphors of his calling—affectionate husband, shining and burning light, hardworking servant—as well as the need for him to fan the flame of genuine piety through spiritual disciplines, he will understand that his task is to communicate his delight in and love for Christ to others. As Edwards put it, the minister "is a 'burning light'; which implies that his spiritual heart and holy ardor is not for himself only, but is communicative and for the benefit of others." As a public person set apart by Christ for a high and holy calling, the pastoral leader engages in every duty of ministerial function with an eye toward stirring his people's hearts toward a passionate love for God.[16]

The Minister's Task

As Edwards conceived it, at the heart of the minister's task is preaching, the ministry of the Word. If the minister is a servant who washes others' feet, he does so by preaching: "This is done by the preaching of the word, which is their main business." In the same way that "priests of old were appointed to blow the silver trumpets, so ministers of the gospel are appointed [to preach the word]." God intends for preaching to accomplish a number of ends, whether serving as "the means God has provided for bringing poor sinners to Christ and salvation by him" or offering correction to false notions of Christianity. Whatever the purpose, Edwards held it as axiomatic that "ministers are set on purpose to explain the word of God, and therefore their people ought to hear them when they offer to explain it to them."[17]

The Substance of Preaching

The substance of the minister's preaching is God's Word and not the dictates of human reason. As Edwards put it in 1750,

---

[16]Ibid., 25:92.

[17]"Christ the Great Example of Gospel Ministers," *WJE*, 25:335; "One Great End in God's Appointing the Gospel Ministry," *WJE*, 25:446, 454; Jonathan Edwards, "Preaching the Gospel Brings Poor Sinners to Christ," in *The Salvation of Souls: Nine Previously Unpublished Sermons on the Call of Ministry and the Gospel*, ed. Richard A. Bailey and Gregory A. Wills (Wheaton, IL: Crossway, 2002), 153.

ministers "are to make the word of God their only rule: their business as ministers of Christ is to preach the word of God, and to that end to give themselves to reading and studying the scriptures." Ministers have been sent on a divine errand. "God has not left it to their discretion what their errand shall be. They are to preach the preaching that he bids them. He has put into their hands a Book containing a summary of doctrine and bids them go and preach that Word." God's Word is not to be interpreted through the grid of natural reason, but "the revelation is to be the rule of its own interpretation." In fact, the Bible contains "a summary of doctrines already discovered and dictated" to ministers; the minister is bound "to preach the dictates of God's infinitely superior understanding, humbly submitting [his] reason as a learner and disciple to that" Word. And yet, he must give to each listener the portion or application of God's Word that meets his or her need. Like a conscientious husbandman, "a faithful minister is careful to give every one his portion of meat and to accommodate his instructions and exhortations to all sorts of persons in all circumstances."[18]

The Manner of Preaching

The minister's manner of preaching is to be fervent. Edwards believed that ministers

> should imitate [Christ] in the manner of his preaching; who taught not as the scribes, but with authority, boldly, zealously, fervently; insisting chiefly on the most important things in religion, being much in warning men of the danger of damnation, setting forth the greatness of the future misery of the ungodly; insisting not only on the outward, but also the inward and spiritual duties of religion.

This fervent approach to preaching is calculated to stir the affections. "I think an exceeding affectionate way of preaching about

---

[18] "One Great End in God's Appointing the Gospel Ministry," *WJE*, 25:447; Jonathan Edwards, "Ministers to Preach Not Their Own Wisdom but the Word of God," in *The Salvation of Souls*, 124, 126, 129; "Sermon on Matt. 13:3–4(a)."

the great things of religion," Edwards noted, "has in itself no tendency to beget false apprehensions of them; but on the contrary a much greater tendency to beget true apprehensions of them than a moderate, dull, indifferent way of speaking of 'em." A fervent manner of delivery

> has so much the greater tendency to beget true ideas or apprehensions in the minds of the hearers, of the subject spoken of, and so to enlighten the understanding: and that for this reason, that such a way or manner of speaking of these things does in fact more truly represent them, than a more cold and indifferent way of speaking of them.

Divine and glorious truths that should move the soul should also move the preacher's manner of presentation.[19]

The Minister's Goal

The reason why the preaching of God's Word is so vital is that the Spirit uses the Word to stir the holy affections of God's people. Reflecting on Luke 24, Edwards observed that when Christ "opened to them the sacred scriptures, he was insisting on the great things that are found written in the word of God." It was this "delightful discourse to the disciples" that caused a "burning of their hearts within them," which was "a sensation sweet." This inward burning represented a "spiritual sense of the truth of divine things," a "spiritual conviction" of God's excellency and glory. And while private reading of God's Word can prove to be "a lively word to the saints [that] has light and heat in it to them," it is particularly the preaching of God's Word that produces this effect.

> God's people sometimes set under the preaching of the Word with ardent and enflamed hearts; there is sometimes a sweet inward ardency of mind under the hearing of the Word. The

---

[19]"Christ the Great Example of Gospel Ministers," *WJE*, 25:339; Jonathan Edwards, "Some Thoughts Concerning the Present Revival of Religion (1742)," in *WJE*, vol. 4, *The Great Awakening*, ed. C. C. Goen (New Haven, CT: Yale University Press, 1972), 386–87.

soul seems as it were to drink in the words of the minister as they come from his mouth, one sentence after another touches their hearts and things are alive, the heart is kindled, there is an inward warmth, the heart is fixed and the affections are active.[20]

This stirring of the affections toward heightened delight in and love for God is the minister's goal. It is not merely a riling of the emotional state of the hearers. Rather, "all affections are raised either by light in the understanding, or by some error and delusion in the understanding." As the light of God's Word appeals to the believer's understanding through preaching, God's Spirit uses his Word to raise the affections. Light and heat must go together in the believer's heart. "Our people don't so much need to have their heads stored, as to have their hearts touched; and they stand in the greatest need of that sort of preaching that has the greatest tendency to do this." Indeed, "holy affections are not heat without light; but evermore arise from some information, some spiritual instruction the mind receives, some light or actual knowledge." The ministry of the Word conveys to the mind "the subject matter of this saving instruction," which is vital for genuine affections.[21]

Yet Edwards well knew that ministers themselves cannot produce genuine affections in the hearts of their people; this is solely the work of God's Spirit. "This inward burning of the heart that we speak of is the exercise of grace in the heart and therefore must be that which is of an holy nature; 'tis the breathing and acting of the Spirit of God in the heart and therefore it must needs be holy and pure." Such should send both minister and people to prayer, asking the Spirit of God to use his Word to produce spiritual fruit.

A people in such a case cry earnestly to that glorious Sun who is the brightness of God's glory and the express image of his

---

[20]Jonathan Edwards, "Sermon on Luke 24:32," in *WJE Online*, vol. 51, *Sermons, Series II, 1736* (Jonathan Edwards Center at Yale University, 2008).
[21]"Some Thoughts Concerning the Present Revival," *WJE*, 4:386, 388; *Religious Affections, WJE*, 2:266; "A Divine and Supernatural Light," *WJE*, 17:416.

person, who is full of light and divine heat, in whom dwells all
the fullness of the Godhead bodily and is more full of spiritual
light and of grace than the sun is of light.

Just as a congregation needs to pray for the Spirit to warm their
hearts, the minister does as well. When a minister seeks the Spirit's
assistance in preaching, he does not receive "immediate suggesting
of words to the apprehension, which may be with a cold dead
heart." Rather, the Spirit's assistance comes "by warming the
heart and filling it with a great sense of those things that are to
be spoken of, and with holy affections, that that sense and those
affections may suggest words."[22]

For it is the Spirit who uses his Word, preached by a minister
whose own affections are moved, to grant a "true sense of the
divine excellency of the things revealed in the Word of God,
and a conviction of the truth and reality of them, thence arising." This happens, as Edwards would later put it in *Religious
Affections*, when "the Spirit of God in his spiritual influences
on the hearts of his saints, operates by infusing or exercising
new, divine and supernatural principles; principles which are
indeed a new and spiritual nature." This spiritual influence,
which is nothing less than a divine communication, produces
"a new inward perception or sensation of their minds" that
enables women and men to see and savor the divine excellency
of Jesus Christ displayed in his Word. This new sense of the heart
causes the believer to "see that God is lovely, and that Christ
is excellent and glorious"; such a sight captivates his heart and
moves him to delight in Christ's beauty as "chief among ten
thousand and altogether lovely." Such delight and joy lead in
turn to new practices of holiness that feed continued delight in
God's glory and beauty.[23]

Such divine light and holy heat, such delight and love to
God in the lives of God's people, are the ultimate goal of the

[22] "Sermon on Luke 24:32"; "Sermon on Matt. 13:3–4(a)"; "Some Thoughts Concerning the Present Revival," *WJE*, 4:437.
[23] "A Divine and Supernatural Light," *WJE*, 17:411–13, 416–17; *Religious Affections*, *WJE*, 2:205, 207, 246, 250.

ministry of the Word, the very reason for which God has granted ministers to his church. They are also why God's people are to attend to biblical preaching. Holy affections have a "tendency" to "cause persons very much to delight in such religious exercises." And it is especially the case with preaching: "It also causes them to delight to hear the Word of God preached: it makes the gospel a joyful sound to them (Ps. 89:15). And makes the feet of those who publish these good things, to be beautiful." That is why God ordained the preaching of God's Word: to impress "divine things on the hearts and affections of men." In fact,

> God hath appointed a particular and lively application of his Word, to men, in the preaching of it, as a fit means to affect sinners, with the importance of the things of religion, and their own misery, and necessity of a remedy, and the glory and sufficiency of a remedy provided; and to stir up the pure minds of the saints, and quicken their affections, by often bringing the great things of religion to their remembrance.

The preaching of God's Word by faithful ministers is a means to "promote those two affections in them," namely, love and joy.[24]

Ultimately, like Christ, ministers are sent to expend themselves "for the salvation and happiness of the souls of men." Called as affectionate husbands, burning and shining lights, hardworking servants, those engaged in the ministry of the Word seek to be used by God's Spirit to preach God's Word in such a lively and passionate way that their hearers' minds and hearts are moved to delight and rejoice in and ardently love Jesus and others. Such is the nature of salvation and happiness—the glorifying and enjoying of God—to which the triune God calls his people for his own glory and infinite happiness.[25]

---

[24]*Religious Affections*, *WJE*, 2:163, 114–15.
[25]Jonathan Edwards, "Christ's Sacrifice an Inducement to His Ministers," in *WJE*, 25:658, 661.

CHAPTER 10

Means of Grace

The Sacraments of Baptism and the Lord's Supper

The controversy that served as the presenting issue in the dissolution of the pastoral relation between Jonathan Edwards and his Northampton congregation focused on the sacraments of baptism and the Lord's Supper. But the controversy involved a great deal more: the nature of popular religion; the structure of Puritan families; the sustenance of New England towns; the relationships between minister and people, church and town; the possibility of discerning regeneration; and the shifting character of authority in colonial America. In order to understand how Edwards viewed baptism and the Lord's Supper, it will be necessary to understand something about the historical background to what became "the qualifications controversy."[1]

---

[1]The best brief account of the "Qualifications Controversy" is George M. Marsden, *Jonathan Edwards: A Life* (New Haven, CT: Yale University Press, 2003), 345–71. See also David D. Hall, "Editor's Introduction," in *The Works of Jonathan Edwards* (hereafter

The Half-Way Covenant and Stoddard's Innovation

In the midst of the tumult caused by the controversy that would ultimately founder his ministry, Edwards wrote to his friend and literary agent, Thomas Foxcroft. "The greatest difficulty of all relating to my principles is here, respecting baptism," he said. "I am not sure but that my people, in length of time and with great difficulty, might be brought to yield the point as to the qualifications for the Lord's Supper, though that is very uncertain. But with respect to the other sacrament, there is scarce any hope of it." As he indicated, both sacraments were involved in Edwards's changing views of admission to the Lord's Table; and the reason for this was buried deep in the moves New England Puritans made to balance the tensions in their own doctrine of the church.[2]

When the Puritans first came to settle Boston colony in 1630, they had limited communicant membership in the church to those who could give a "relation" of spiritual experience. Those who could testify to being regenerated were admitted to the Lord's Supper, and they also were granted two other valuable privileges: the right to have their children baptized and the right to vote. For the first generation, who desired to create a "godly commonwealth," only those who were guided by God's Spirit should have a voice in political as well as ecclesiastical affairs. And their children gained the particular privilege of growing up within the bounds of the church. Because of this and because the vast majority of that first generation could testify to spiritual renewal, the church was able to be both pure and comprehensive: it was made up of professing believers and their children, and it encompassed the vast majority of the colony.[3]

WJE), vol. 12, *Ecclesiastical Writings* (New Haven, CT: Yale University Press, 1992), 1–86, and Anne S. Brown and David D. Hall, "Family Strategies and Religious Practice: Baptism and the Lord's Supper in Early New England," in *Lived Religion in America: Toward a History of Practice*, ed. David D. Hall (Princeton, NJ: Princeton University Press, 1997), 41–68.

[2] Jonathan Edwards to Thomas Foxcroft, May 24, 1749, in *WJE*, vol. 16, *Letters and Personal Writings*, ed. George S. Claghorn (New Haven, CT: Yale University Press, 1998), 283.

[3] The account that follows largely summarizes E. Brooks Holifield, *The Covenant Sealed: The Development of Puritan Sacramental Theology in Old and New England, 1570–1720* (New Haven, CT: Yale University Press, 1974); Mark Noll, *America's God: From*

However, as the second generation grew up within the bounds of the church and became adults, they could not testify to a work of regeneration in their own hearts. As they failed to step forward for communicant membership (and for the right of suffrage in the colony's governance), the concern to maintain a comprehensive church turned to the third generation: on what basis would the grandchildren of the founding generation be baptized and so included in the life of the church? Seventeenth-century New England ministers argued that this third generation, the children of baptized-but-noncommunicant members who were essentially moral and orthodox, were also included within the church covenant and so should be baptized as well. Opponents derisively called this "the Half-Way Covenant."

While the ministers had discovered a means to maintain the comprehensive nature of the church, including the grandchildren of the founders in it, they also had a means to maintain the purity of the church: they continued to restrict full, communicant membership to those who could give a testimony of spiritual renewal. Part of the difficulty with this arrangement, though, was the continued linkage between communicant membership and suffrage. As new generations came, through birth and immigration, fewer and fewer people could vote on the political matters that affected them. A solution came from a minister in a frontier town, Solomon Stoddard. The second minister in Northampton, Massachusetts, Stoddard argued that it was simply not possible to discern regeneration and weed out hypocrites. Therefore, the threshold for the admission to the Lord's Supper should be changed and made essentially the same as that required for one's children to be baptized: an individual simply needed to be moral, orthodox, and sincere.

The result was that Stoddard broke the linkage between spiritual regeneration and political suffrage. Everyone was qualified to vote in political matters because everyone could become a communicant member. But while it appeared that the desire to

---

Jonathan Edwards to Abraham Lincoln (New York: Oxford University Press, 2002), 31–50; Robert G. Pope, *The Half-Way Covenant: Church Membership in Puritan New England* (Princeton, NJ: Princeton University Press, 1969).

maintain a comprehensive church won the day, Stoddard sought to maintain his commitment to a pure church through intense revivalistic preaching and close pastoral care. In addition, he was persuaded that the Lord's Supper is a "converting" ordinance; as a means of grace, it should be offered to all as a potential vehicle for conversion. As a result, Stoddard transformed the "Half-Way Covenant" into a new way of linking town and church, family and religion.[4]

This was the context within which Edwards forged his understanding of baptism and the Lord's Supper as means of grace to sustain the Christian life. And while he would operate within this framework for a significant length of time, his thought about the sacraments—from his earliest days in ministry—would lead him on a collision course with this received tradition. Inasmuch as he was Stoddard's grandson and was ministering in the frontier town where "Stoddardism" was established, it was inevitable that the collision would be messy.

Baptism

Before exploring how Edwards played out his understanding of the sacraments in the fires of controversy, it may be helpful first to see what he said about each sacrament in less intense times. Like most Reformed theologians, Edwards based his understanding of baptism, and especially infant baptism, on his prior understanding of God's covenant. "When God admits children into covenant with their parents, and so admits 'em to be the subjects of the visible seal of the covenant," he commented on Genesis 18:18–19, "it is as it were on a dependence on the future religion and piety of those children as so ordinarily consequent on it, that it may be looked upon as virtually included in it." Just as God sealed the covenant he made with his people at Sinai "by baptizing them by water out of the cloud," so he does with his people today.[5]

---

[4]See Paul R. Lucas, "'The Death of the Prophet Lamented': The Legacy of Solomon Stoddard," in *Jonathan Edwards's Writings: Text, Context, Interpretation*, ed. Stephen J. Stein (Bloomington: Indiana University Press, 1996), 69–84.

[5]Jonathan Edwards, "Genesis 18:18–19," in *WJE*, vol. 24, *The Blank Bible*, ed. Stephen J. Stein (New Haven, CT: Yale University Press, 2006), 161; Jonathan Edwards, "Notes

Baptism serves as "a sign and seal" of "admission" into "the visible kingdom of Christ." As a result, baptism is "the sacrament of initiation" that parallels the Lord's Supper as the sacrament of "confirmation." There is an element of profession in baptism; it is a profession of religion, of being called by the Lord's name. "And so by this swearing, they come into the name of God, as persons, when they make profession of religion by baptism, are said to be baptized into the name of Father, Son, and Holy Ghost." That is why our children are baptized into the Trinitarian name; they are "devoted" to God in this way. Such baptism does not require immersion as "the Anabaptists" argued. Rather, "baptism, with washing only, without plunging, does represent that which is often compared to a dying or being buried with Christ, viz. our being cleansed from sin." In fact, "pouring" serves as a better sign to the outpouring of the Holy Spirit, Edwards thought. "It seems to me much the most probable, therefore, that John baptized by affusion, and not by dipping or plunging; and that so there was a greater agreement between the type and antitype that were then conjoined, than there would have been if John had baptized by dipping."[6]

Edwards was careful to say that baptism does not require or produce regeneration. Concerning "whether or no all that are regularly admitted to baptism are spiritually regeneration," Edwards wrote, "No. The Apostle and other inspired persons baptized many adult persons that were hypocrites, but they were regularly admitted to baptism. . . . But if an adult person may be regularly admitted to baptism, and regeneration not be connected with it, I don't see why an infant mayn't." At this point, in reflections written before 1733, Edwards was ready to argue that even parents who are "a Christian only visibly and not really" may bring their children to be baptized. The benefit of baptism is not

on Scripture, no. 210," in *WJE*, vol. 15, *Notes on Scripture*, ed. Stephen J. Stein (New Haven, CT: Yale University Press, 1998), 139.
[6]Jonathan Edwards, "Matthew 28:18–19," in *WJE*, 24:878; "Notes on Scripture, no. 468," *WJE*, 15:557, 559; "1 Corinthians 12:13," *WJE*, 24:1053; "Romans 6:4," *WJE*, 24:1001; Jonathan Edwards, "The 'Miscellanies,' no. 694," in *WJE*, vol. 18, *The "Miscellanies," 501–832*, ed. Ava Chamberlain (New Haven, CT: Yale University Press, 2000), 276.

simply to the children, but also to the parents. "If the parents do sincerely, believingly and entirely, with a thorough disposition, will and desire, dedicate their child to God that they bring to baptism, if that child dies in infancy, the parents have good grounds to hope for its salvation," Edwards thought. And if the child survives to adulthood, they have grounds to hope "that the blessing of God will attend their thorough care and pains to bring up their child in the nurture and admonition of the Lord."[7]

The main thrust of what Edwards taught concerning baptism was that parents offer or dedicate their children to God and so promise to raise them in the nurture and admonition of the Lord. As Edwards told his people in a 1748 lecture, in baptism parents take on an obligation, "a solemn vow," to raise their children to embrace the gospel. This reflects what he had noted several years earlier in his "Miscellanies":

> If a parent did sincerely and with his whole heart dedicate his child to God, he will afterward take thorough and effectual care in bringing up his children in the nurture and admonition of the Lord, continuing in prayer and dependence on God for them; and in that way it is sealed to them, that ordinarily they shall obtain success.[8]

Lord's Supper

While it does not appear that Edwards preached any sermons directly on baptism, he preached a number of sermons on foundational texts on the Lord's Supper. That was to be expected; because of the regularity of the Lord's Supper in the worship of the church, it was fitting for him to do so. But the circumstances of New England Christianity made it necessary as well. Because any baptized individual who was orthodox, moral, and sincere could be admitted to the sacrament, Edwards felt the need to

---

[7] "The 'Miscellanies,' no. 577," *WJE*, 18:114–15.
[8] Jonathan Edwards, "Sermon on Eph. 6:4," in *WJE Online*, vol. 66, *Sermons, Series II, 1748* (Jonathan Edwards Center at Yale University, 2008), L. 6r. col. 2.; "The 'Miscellanies,' no. 595," *WJE*, 18:129.

teach carefully about what the meal was and to preach insistently on what a worthy reception of it looked like.

One of the things that Edwards stressed in his preaching on the Lord's Supper was that the sacrament provides participation in or communion with Christ.

> [For] true believers, hence, communion [is] a joint participation by receiving by faith. By faith the soul accepts [Christ's benefits]. As it were, [the soul] reaches out the hand and takes, receives, as its food, i.e. its proper good; i.e. receives as its refreshment, as its sweet satisfying enjoyment, as its nourishment; as its strength, comfort.[9]

More strikingly, Edwards suggested that in the Lord's Supper, Christians have communion with Christ. "The head and members, they partake together of the same life and health," he declared. Just as a parent and his children sit down to a meal and partake the same food, "so Christ when he invites his people to the Gospel feast so he sits with them at the Table." Especially, Christ shares the benefits that he gained through his obedience and satisfaction.

> He has justification from sin by his death, he becoming our surety. Our iniquities were laid upon him; he was made sin for us; he had our guilt laid upon him and thereby stood obliged to suffer the penalty of the law, but by his suffering he was freed from this guilt. And when God the Father released him from the prison of the grave, then he was justified as having suffered enough to answer the imputed guilt that lay upon him. So he is rewarded for his own obedience of which the offering up his body and blood was the greatest act.

As a result, believers have communion with Christ's own justification; the sign and seal of that reality is the Lord's Supper:

---

[9]Jonathan Edwards, "Sermon on 1 Cor. 10:16(b)," in *WJE Online*, vol. 63, *Sermons, Series II, 1745* (Jonathan Edwards Center at Yale University, 2008). There were no page numbers or references to cite.

"Believers in their being justified from sin by Christ's death and having eternal life by his obedience, they have fellowship with Christ in his own sacrifice."[10]

The language of participation and communion finds its theological counterpart in the idea of "union." The feasting of the Lord's Supper is an expression of believers' union with Christ. "There is the nearest union and a holy friendship between Christ and believers," Edwards said.

> Feasting together betokens love and friendship. . . . So 'tis from the wonderful love of Jesus Christ that sinners are called to this feast and that he has provided such a feast for them at so dear a rate. This love is without a parallel, and all those that do accept of the invitation that are truly his guests, their hearts are possessed with a spirit of true love to Christ. . . . There is true love between Christ and his guests.[11]

Edwards forcefully rejected the Roman Catholic understanding of transubstantiation, which he viewed as "monstrous." As he put it, "There is no such thing as our partaking of the body and blood of Christ in a proper sense. The end of the sacrament is not that we may eat the flesh and drink the blood of Christ without a metaphor." Rather, when Christians speak of eating the body and blood of Jesus, they mean the spiritual benefits procured by Christ's body and blood. Receiving these spiritual benefits by faith is rightly compared to eating bread and drinking wine, he held.

> It is by faith in that body and blood, or in that sacrifice, receiving of it and applying it to ourselves and depending upon it that we receive those benefits. This faith and dependence on the body and blood for the benefits is as it were eating and drinking his body and blood in order to satisfaction and nourishment.

---

[10]Jonathan Edwards, "Sermons on 1 Cor. 10:16(a)," in *WJE Online*, vol. 45, *Sermons, Series II, 1729–1731* (Jonathan Edwards Center at Yale University, 2008), L. 5r–L. 5v.
[11]Jonathan Edwards, "The Spirit Blessings of the Gospel Represented by a Feast," in *WJE*, vol. 14, *Sermons and Discourses, 1723–1729*, ed. Kenneth P. Minkema (New Haven, CT: Yale University Press, 1997), 286.

The elements of bread and wine serve as "sensible signs" that represent these spiritual realities. As such, these two elements function well: bread is the food that has a "wholesome nourishing strengthening nature"; wine, "spiritual life [and] vigor." And so, the spiritual feasting of the supper strengthens and provides spiritual vigor to those who participate.[12]

The Lord's Supper is not only a communion with Christ in his benefits. It is also a communion with other believers, both here on earth and in heaven. For Christians, the Lord's Supper is a sign of their common union with Jesus. "Having one spiritual husband to whom they are lawfully espoused, it follows that they all together constitute one spouse of Christ," Edwards said. And so, the Lord's Supper should be testimony to "a sweet harmony among all the members as to temper and as to conversation; and a natural inclination to sweet society and mutual converse to one with another." Edwards extended this "communion of the saints" to heaven itself. As he put it in an early sermon on 1 Corinthians 10:16, "The Lord's Supper therefore is designed that the church on earth might have communion with the church in heaven that they might be partakers of the same spiritual food in a lesser degree here in this world and that they might by means of it be brought to the same perfection." Our confidence is that "all true members of Christ's church here, they have communion with the church in glory in God's ordinances."[13]

In order to come to the table and participate in such great gospel mysteries, it is necessary for people to examine themselves. In 1731, Edwards preached a sermon on 1 Corinthians 11:28–29, in which he stressed that "persons ought to examine themselves of their fitness before they presume to partake of the Lord's Supper, lest by their unworthy partaking, they eat and drink damnation to themselves." And a person's examination should center on "whether or no he lives in any known sin" and

---

[12] "Sermon on 1 Cor. 10:16(a)," L. 3r., L. 4r., L. 6v., L. 7r.
[13] Jonathan Edwards, "Sacramental Union in Christ," in *WJE*, vol. 25, *Sermons and Discourses, 1743–1758*, ed. Wilson H. Kimnach (New Haven, CT: Yale University Press, 2006), 585, 586; "Sermon on 1 Cor. 10:16(a)," L. 6r–L. 6v.

whether he has sinned against a neighbor or bears a "spirit of hatred or envy or revenge" toward him. Those who come to the supper unrepentant, with unconfessed sin, demonstrate "a horrid contempt of the ordinance and the things signified in it." Such is "the most horrid dissimulation and mockery," promising to "own the covenant" in the supper, but "never so much as seriously to purpose any such thing," and in fact, being determined to "go on in the indulgence of their filthy lusts." Those who eat this meal in this fashion bring God's judgment on themselves, both now and hereafter.[14]

Not only should there be self-examination, but also there should be a concerted remembrance of the person and work of Christ during the supper. When Christ directed his disciples to do this meal in his remembrance, that meant "that we should do it to renew and assist our thoughts and meditations of Christ. Not only to keep alive the memory of the Cross of Christ in the world, but to revive the thoughts of Christ in particular." This would lead to "suitable exercises of the heart toward him in our hearts" with the renewal of "suitable affections." And these renewed affections would lead professing believers to give themselves "entirely unto Jesus Christ, making a solemn renewed dedication of ourselves to him." The Lord's Supper serves the Christian life by causing believers to forsake sin and turn wholeheartedly to Jesus.[15]

For those who eat and drink in a worthy manner, the Lord's Supper is a sign and seal of a final, eschatological meal. In 1733, Edwards argued that "the saints shall hereafter as it were eat and drink with Christ at his table [in] his kingdom of glory." Because Christ is already exalted at the right hand of the Father, and because Christ is already enjoying the blessings of his reward for accomplishing the work of redemption, saints shall one day fully and finally join Christ and participate in his glory. "They shall be present with him in the highest sense and most imme-

[14]Jonathan Edwards, "Self-examination and the Lord's Supper," in *WJE*, vol. 17, *Sermons and Discourses, 1730–1733*, ed. Mark Valeri (New Haven, CT: Yale University Press, 1999), 266, 267, 268, 270, 271.
[15]Jonathan Edwards, "Sermon on Luke 22:19," in *WJE Online*, vol. 49, *Sermons, Series II, 1734* (Jonathan Edwards Center at Yale University, 2008), L. 4r., L. 5r.

diate manner," he said. "This is intimated in their eating and drinking with him at his Table." And believers have a foretaste of that future intimate fellowship now as they participate in the supper. "In that ordinance, we may have the foretaste of that eternal feast with Christ in glory. That spiritual food is afforded us in the Lord's Supper and is given to the worthy partakers is a foretaste and earnest of that future happiness."[16]

Qualifications

While Edwards freely admitted that he had continued the practices of his grandfather—both in the Half-Way Covenant and in open communion—he also claimed that he was long uncomfortable with the practices. In the early 1730s, in his private notebooks, he began working out his understanding of what makes someone "a visible saint." He started with the premise that "to be a visible Christian is to appear to be a real Christian in the eye of a public Christian judgment, and to have a right in Christian reason and according to Christian rules to be received and treated as such." The problem is that there are a number of people who do not give an indication one way or another whether they are "real Christians." How should the church regard them? "The Christian church should indeed use all proper means to discriminate true Christians from others, that is, the strictest trials that would not be likely to shut out multitudes that are true Christians."[17]

But what rules would be acceptable? "The gospel rule seems to be, to receive those that make a profession of a hearty believing the truth of the gospel, and a walking in all the ordinances and according to the moral rules of the gospel." And what does "a hearty believing the truth of the gospel" look like? Those who profess belief

---

[16]Jonathan Edwards, "Sermon on Luke 22:30," in *WJE Online*, vol. 48, *Sermons, Series II, 1733* (Jonathan Edwards Center at Yale University, 2008), L. 2v., L. 4v., L. 5r.
[17]Jonathan Edwards, "The 'Miscellanies,' no. 335," in *WJE*, vol. 13, *The "Miscellanies," a–500*, ed. Thomas A. Schafer (New Haven, CT: Yale University Press, 1994), 441; "The 'Miscellanies,' no. 338," *WJE*, 13:413.

must examine and prove themselves, whether or no they believe the gospel with all their hearts, or are heartily convinced of the truth of it; and whether or no they are brought thoroughly to forsake all the ways of sin, to deny every lust, and live in the performance of all Christ's commands universally; and whether they are fully and seriously determined so to do to the end, through all opposition; and whether they live in charity with all Christians without entertaining any malicious or revengeful spirit towards any, but on the contrary loving them and seeking their good.

Here was a standard far beyond what Grandfather Stoddard had required: such a profession and lifestyle would mean that "visible Christians" are as close to "real Christians" as one can determine.[18]

After someone is admitted to the table, based on such a profession, they should be frequently reminded "of the danger of hypocrisy, and to have the signs of hypocrites laid before them." Self-examination should be regular, and if self-examination leads to the discovery of one's own hypocrisy, there is still the possibility of conversion. While the church inevitably will admit some who are hypocrites, Edwards believed that the onus should be on the individual seeking admission to the church. "If he knows that he lives in wickedness, he don't do regularly in coming, nor can he think that God accepts him, nor can he expect any blessing with ordinances, but a curse."[19]

The benefit of this way of approaching the matter is that the wicked "would visibly be separate from Christ, in that they are separate from the church, and don't come to join themselves." As a result, they would have a clear sense of their position under the preaching of the Word; "they would lie abundantly more open to conviction and to the force of the calls and motives of the gospel." In addition, they would be "denied all privileges while keeping away from the Supper, of having their children baptized, etc."

---

[18] "The 'Miscellanies,' no. 338," *WJE*, 13:413; "The 'Miscellanies,' no. 462," *WJE*, 13:503.
[19] "The 'Miscellanies,' no. 462," *WJE*, 13:505; "The 'Miscellanies,' no. 689," *WJE*, 18:259.

Such lines help the church maintain its purity on the one hand and provide a better position to preach the gospel on the other.[20]

These private reflections about the qualifications for admission to the table and the nature of Christian profession worked their way out publicly. Perhaps the most important public statement was in Edwards's *Religious Affections*. There, he answered the question, "What profession may properly be called a profession of Christianity?" Boiled down, he said, "For a man to profess Christianity is for him to declare that he has it." This involves not only intellectual commitments, but heart ones as well.

> Thus it is essential to Christianity that we repent of our sins, that we be convinced of our own sinfulness, and that we are sensible we have justly exposed ourselves to God's wrath, and that our hearts do renounce all sin, and that we do with our whole hearts embrace Christ as our own Savior, and that we love him above all, and are willing for his sake to forsake all, and that we do give up ourselves to be entirely and forever his.

And this profession of the reality of these things should be joined with some evidence of Christian practice. Merely because someone is "an honest man and a moral man" does not mean that he has a solid profession of faith. The Christian practice that serves as evidence of a credible profession of faith is holy living, behavior that follows the example of Christ, the Sermon on the Mount, the Ten Commandments, and other scriptural rules.[21]

When Edwards finally determined to act on this understanding of what a credible profession of faith looks like as terms for admission to the table, a firestorm broke out. And based on the larger context, one could see why. In proposing to change the terms of admission to communicant membership, Edwards was not simply changing the pathway to full membership in the church. He was also limiting access to infant baptism. Only those who could make a credible profession and who were admitted to

---

[20]"The 'Miscellanies,' no. 462," *WJE*, 13:505.
[21]Jonathan Edwards, *WJE*, vol. 2, *Religious Affections*, ed. John E. Smith (New Haven, CT: Yale University Press, 1959), 413.

the Lord's Supper could have their children baptized. Clearly, that was the motive of many for being communicant church members, as Edwards observed in a 1731 sermon on the Lord's Supper:

> The ordinance was appointed for [the] spiritual good of the partakers; if those, therefore, that come don't seek that in it, and 'tis not [from] any desire of their spiritual good or from any conscientious regard to God's command that they come, but only for some end, some temporal advance or credit, or merely that their children mayn't lie under the disgrace of being unbaptized, they eat and drink unworthily.

And so, not only was this a change in church membership—it was also a change that would overthrow the family structure that had regulated Puritan family life for hundreds of years.[22]

But it did something more: by excluding those who were not able to make a credible profession of faith, it would undo the "comprehensive ideal" that was at the heart of the Puritan vision. One could say that in working out the tension between the ideal of the church's purity and its comprehension of all town members, Edwards came to a different answer than did his grandfather. While Stoddard's innovation forsook purity in favor of comprehension, Edwards's new direction forsook comprehension for purity. It was more important that the visible church be made up of visible saints whose professions were credible, and their children, instead of a visible church that was made up of all the members of the town, whose professions were irregular and whose lives were impure. While Edwards's position would have made him comfortable with modern-day conservative Presbyterians, it put him out of step with the church and town of his day. As a result, it also served as the presenting issue of his dismissal as pastor in Northampton in 1750.

---

[22] "Self-examination and the Lord's Supper," *WJE*, 17:269.

CHAPTER 11

Means of Grace

Prayer, Personal and Global

When Jonathan Edwards was a young man, prayer was central to his understanding of the Christian life. "Prayer seemed to be natural to me; as the breath, by which the inward burnings of my heart had vent," he reflected later in life. He remembered times when he "used to spend abundance of my time, in walking alone in the woods and solitary places, for meditation, soliloquy and prayer, and converse with God. . . . [I] was almost constantly in ejaculatory prayer, wherever I was." But this was not simply a young man's concern. Perhaps his last sermon preached, upon his departure from Stockbridge, Massachusetts, in January 1758, Edwards exhorted his people to "watch and pray always that we may be thought worthy {to stand before Christ}." From the beginning to the end of his Christian life, prayer was a vital means of God's grace in sustaining the Christian life.[1]

Not only is prayer necessary for sustaining a life of personal discipleship, but it also should be global. Edwards would repeatedly point to the necessity of prayer for the advancement of Christ's kingdom and the bringing of millennial glory. In 1747, in response to requests from his Scottish correspondents to advance the cause of worldwide revival and evangelization, Edwards published *An Humble Attempt to Promise Explicit Agreement and Visible Union of God's People in Extraordinary Prayer for the Revival of Religion and the Advancement of Christ's Kingdom on Earth.* At the heart of his argument was that God uses prayer to advance the history of the work of redemption. Scripture gives

> an account of *how* this future glorious advancement of the church should be brought on, or introduced; viz. by great multitudes in different towns and countries taking up a *joint resolution*, and coming into an express and visible *agreement*, that they will, by united and extraordinary *prayer*, seek to God that he would come and manifest himself, and grant the tokens and fruits of his gracious presence.

Prayer is a duty for advancing God's kingdom.[2]

These twin foci—the personal and global—merged together seamlessly for Edwards in prayer throughout his entire life. Both served to ignite his affections and stir them to seek God and ways that increased delight in God. In his "Personal Narrative," written around 1739 or 1740 for his son-in-law, Aaron Burr, he noted how "my heart has been much on the advancement of Christ's Kingdom of the world. The histories of the past advancement of Christ's Kingdom have been sweet to me." He commented that

[1]Jonathan Edwards, "Personal Narrative," in *The Works of Jonathan Edwards* (hereafter *WJE*), vol. 16, *Letters and Personal Writings*, ed. George S. Claghorn (New Haven, CT: Yale University Press, 1998), 794; Jonathan Edwards, "Watch and Pray Always," in *WJE*, vol. 25, *Sermons and Discourses, 1743–1758*, ed. Wilson H. Kimnach (New Haven, CT: Yale University Press, 2006), 716.
[2]Jonathan Edwards, "An Humble Attempt," in *WJE*, vol. 5, *Apocalyptic Writings*, ed. Stephen J. Stein (New Haven, CT: Yale University Press, 1977), 314.

upon reading anything on this theme, "I have lotted upon it all the way as I read. And my mind has been much entertained and delighted." But in the next paragraphs, he described a time when he wandered into the woods to pray and he had a view "of the glory of the Son of God," and the excellency of that sight given in prayer was overwhelming. Keeping these two themes together— the personal and global—is vital for understanding how prayer advances the Christian life.[3]

Affectionate Prayer

Like the preaching of God's Word and the sacraments, prayer is a means by which holy affections are stirred, in Edwards's view. In prayer, Christians do not adore God's attributes in order to inform him of what is true about him. Nor do they argue with God in such a way to incline his heart and persuade him to show mercy. Rather, the purpose of prayer is "to affect our own hearts with the things we express, and so to prepare us to receive the blessings we ask." As the heart is duly affected and stirred to seek God's glory in a disinterested fashion, then it is in a place best calculated to receive its desires. Prayer is one of God's appointed means that "has a tendency deeply to affect the hearts of those who attend these means."[4]

Part of the reason for this is that God delights to give his people clearer views of himself in prayer. "While they are praying, he gives them sweet views of his glorious grace, purity, sufficiency, and sovereignty; and enables them, with great quietness, to rest in him, to leave themselves and their prayers with him, submitting to his will, and trusting in his grace and faithfulness," Edwards declared. God gives his children every blessing in response to prayer, and especially, the communication of himself.[5]

[3]I have learned much on Edwards and prayer from Peter Beck, *The Voice of Faith: Jonathan Edwards's Theology of Prayer* (Guelph, ON: Joshua, 2010).
[4]Jonathan Edwards, *WJE*, vol. 2, *Religious Affections*, ed. John E. Smith (New Haven, CT: Yale University Press, 1959), 115, 121.
[5]Jonathan Edwards, "The Most High a Prayer-Hearing God," in *The Works of Jonathan Edwards*, ed. Edward Hickman, 2 vols. (1834; repr., Carlisle, PA: Banner of Truth, 1974), 2:114; Jonathan Edwards, "The Terms of Prayer," in *WJE*, vol. 19, *Sermons and Discourses, 1734–1738*, ed. M. X. Lesser (New Haven, CT: Yale University Press, 2001), 783.

The language of prayer is natural to those who have received the new sense of the heart. "'Tis plain from the Scripture," Edwards wrote, "that it is the tendency of true grace to cause persons very much to delight in such religious exercises." And so it was that "grace made Daniel delight in the duty of prayer, and solemnly to attend it three times a day: as it also did David." The Spirit himself assists the believer in prayer "by warming the heart and filling it with a great sense of those things that are to be spoken of, and with holy affections, that that sense and those affections may suggest words."[6]

Prayer is thus the result of the new sense of the heart, the new disposition that the Holy Spirit infuses so that God's people may act in new holy ways. Or to put it differently, "faith is that inward sense and act of which prayer is the expression." Those hearts that have inclined themselves toward God have new dispositions and desires for God and are filled with faith in God expressed through prayer. "Faith in God is expressed in praying to God. Faith in the Lord Jesus Christ is expressed in praying to Christ and praying in the name of Christ, and the promises are made to asking in Christ's name in the same manner as they are to believing in Christ." The new sense of the heart, granted by the gracious work of the Spirit and expressed in faith, leads those who receive it to pray.[7]

That said, prayer is not in itself an infallible sign of grace. It is striking that Edwards wrote far more in *Religious Affections* about hypocritical prayer than about genuine prayer. Just because someone spends a great deal of time in prayer does not mean that he or she has known a genuine work of grace. Hypocrites may "abound in the external duties of religion, such as prayer, hearing the Word preached, singing and religious conference." In addition, "false religion may cause persons to be loud and

---

[6]*Religious Affections*, WJE, 2:163; Jonathan Edwards, "Some Thoughts Concerning the Present Revival of Religion (1742)," in WJE, vol. 4, *The Great Awakening*, ed. C. C. Goen (New Haven, CT: Yale University Press, 1972), 437.

[7]Jonathan Edwards, "Writings on Faith," no. 85, in WJE, vol. 21, *Writings on the Trinity, Grace, and Faith*, ed. Sang Hyun Lee (New Haven, CT: Yale University Press, 2003), 438, 439.

earnest in prayer" or use bold and confident language in prayer. Simply because others notice "a man that boldly calls God his Father, and commonly speaks in the most bold, familiar, and appropriating language in prayer, 'My Father, my dear Redeemer, my sweet Savior, my Beloved,' and the like" does not mean that there has been genuine conversion or real grace. Moreover, freedom of speech in prayer does not serve as a true sign of grace. Though those who experience such freedom of expression may call it "God's being with them," this may arise from other ways "besides God's spiritual presence."[8]

Not only do hypocrites pray in a way that evidences a lack of grace; even genuine believers can pray in a false manner. A general rule for all Christian obedience, Edwards believed, is "that duty which is not done in sincerity, is not done at all in the sight of God; for [God] looks not at words or sounds, but at the heart." And so, if a Christian makes "a mere pretense of prayer," that is not real prayer. Nor is it real prayer in God's sight if "it is not made with a humble sense of their unworthiness of what is prayed for, and a submissive sense of its being something that is in God's free disposal." Likewise, it is false prayer when one "directs his words to God, but at the same time looks, it may be, to himself, or to the creature, or looks to nothing at all." Prayer that is dominated by "unbelief and discouragement" is not real prayer. Finally, prayers that "don't beg, but demand" from God, evidencing a heart that is not dependent upon God's mercy, but insistent upon his desert, are false prayers.[9]

By contrast, genuine prayer has certain marks as well. Obviously, some of the marks are the opposite of the false attitudes that negate prayer. So, genuine prayer is sincere and heartfelt; it is characterized by humility and submission; it looks to God completely with confident belief and encouragement, even as it begs God for grace, strength, and comfort. It is also characterized by a genuine sense of dependence upon God. That is a major reason

---

[8]*Religious Affections*, WJE, 2:183, 164, 170–71, 269.
[9]"The Terms of Prayer," WJE, 19:786, 787, 788.

why God has given us prayer as a means of securing his mercy; it serves his glory by casting believers in dependence upon him.

> That we, when we desire to receive any mercy from him, should humbly supplicate the Divine Being for the bestowment of that mercy, is but a suitable acknowledgement of our dependence on the power and mercy of God for that which we need, and but a suitable honor paid to the great Author and Fountain of all good.[10]

Above all, genuine prayer is mediated by Christ to the Father. God is ready to hear the prayers of his people because they have a "glorious Mediator." Through his death on the cross, Christ "has purchased this privilege, viz., that the prayers of those who believe in him should be heard." Jesus merited this privilege for his children. "Our prayers would be of no account, and of no avail with God, were it not for the merits of Christ." Even more, Christ is present at the Father's right hand to "enforce the prayers of his people, by his intercession." Jesus has entered into the presence of God, by means of his own bloody sacrifice, in order to present Christians' prayers to the Father. Those who pray genuinely have this confidence: "We are sure that we shall be accepted when we come in his name."[11]

And true prayer runs to God through Christ in order to have desires fulfilled. Edwards notes that human desires "are naturally very large. 'Tis no small matter will satisfy the desires of the soul of man: 'tis not all the enjoyments of a finite world will do it." The Christian's desires are not slackened by regeneration; while godliness may "regulate" his or her desire, it does not diminish desire. The difference between the Christian and the natural man or woman is this: the Christian knows where and how to direct desires. "God's people's desires of happiness are exceeding extensive; but as extensive as they are, there is great encouragement in this doctrine to go to God with them. They may expose as

---

[10]"The Most High a Prayer-Hearing God," 116.
[11]Ibid.; Jonathan Edwards, "Christ's Sacrifice," in *WJE*, vol. 10, *Sermons and Discourses, 1720–1723*, ed. Wilson H. Kimnach (New Haven, CT: Yale University Press, 1992), 602.

large desires as they will, God is ready to hear them. God stands ready to give 'em their hearts' desires." God delights to allow his people to draw near to him and to satisfy themselves in him, which in turn increases their desires for him. "Having tasted of little," Edwards notes, "makes 'em desire much."[12]

Prayer Revival

Because prayer arises from holy affections and serves to stir and renew them, it is no wonder that revival is a means of both renewing and increasing prayer. One of the great effects of the outpouring of God's Spirit in Northampton was increased attention to the means of grace in general and prayer in particular. In *Some Thoughts Concerning the Present Revival of Religion in New England*, published in 1742, Edwards noted an increase of prayer that characterized many who were being spiritually renewed. One particular man who was growing in grace, "through great trials and conflicts, and long continued struggling and fighting with sin, and *earnest and constant prayer* and labor in religion, and engagedness of mind in the use of all means, attended with a great exactness of life." For the congregation as a whole, there was such compassion upon the lost, "that would allow of no support or rest, but in going to God, and pouring out the soul in prayer for them." Above all, believers felt they had "a wonderful access to God by prayer, as it were seeing him, and sensibly immediately conversing with him, as much oftentimes (to use the person's own expressions) as if Christ were here on earth, sitting on a visible throne to be approached to and conversed with."[13]

And yet, though such renewed prayer was the characteristic of the revival period, Edwards longed for his people to pray even more fervently for the outpouring of God's Spirit. In November 1740, a month after George Whitefield had preached at Northampton and had moved the congregation to tears, Edwards preached at a public fast day. In his sermon, he urged his con-

---

[12] "The Terms of Prayer," *WJE*, 19:784, 785.
[13] Jonathan Edwards, "Faithful Narrative of the Surprising Work of God," in *WJE*, 4:161; "Some Thoughts Concerning the Present Revival," *WJE*, 4:334, 340.

gregation to pray for an outpouring of God's Spirit: "I am bold to say that God is now offering the blessing of his Holy Spirit to this town, and I am bold to say we may have it only for asking." If the people of Northampton would earnestly "cry to God for the renewed pouring out of his Holy Spirit upon us," then God would answer their prayers: "Doubtless we may have it, if we will." Edwards longed for the renewed awakening, sparked by Whitefield's preaching, to take hold; but this was the work of the Spirit and prayer.[14]

Even after the awakening had apparently come to an end, Edwards still urged Christians to pray for the outpouring of the Spirit. The recent days, he suggested, should "excite them to pray for the continuance and increase, and greater extent of such blessings . . . to pray for the outpouring of his Spirit and the carrying on this work." Edwards was firmly committed to the principle that "it is God's will, through his wonderful grace, that the prayers of his saints should be one great and principal means of carrying on the designs of Christ's kingdom in the world." The times called for not just ordinary prayer, but extraordinary: prayer accompanied by fasting, begging God to cast the demonic enemy out of the land and to save sinners for his glory. And this prayer should be offered especially for the ministers of the land, that they would be granted "much greater degrees" of the presence of God to accompany their ministries.[15]

The best way to ask for the outpouring of God's Spirit was for groups of people, congregations, and especially ministers to covenant together to pray at specific times. The entire congregation could spend whole days in prayer and fasting, both at the church house and in various homes. These smaller "praying companies or societies" would serve "to animate and engage devotion more," to stir the heart to engage with God to a greater degree.

---

[14]Jonathan Edwards, "Praying for the Spirit," in *WJE*, vol. 22, *Sermons and Discourses, 1739–1742*, ed. Harry S. Stout and Nathan O. Hatch, with Kyle Farley (New Haven, CT: Yale University Press, 2003), 220–21. For Whitefield's visit to Northampton, see George M. Marsden, *Jonathan Edwards: A Life* (New Haven, CT: Yale University Press, 2003), 203–13.

[15]"Some Thoughts Concerning the Present Revival," *WJE*, 4:516, 519.

In Northampton, the congregation had been broken up into these smaller societies, which met at different times during the day, at morning, noon, and evening. This was "of great benefit to assist and engage the minds of the people" in prayer.[16]

Likewise, all of God's people across a given nation should covenant together to pray at specific times for revival and renewal. Edwards broached the idea of a prayer union in *Some Thoughts Concerning the Present Revival of Religion*: "I have often thought it would be a thing very desirable, and very likely to be followed with a great blessing, if there could be some contrivance that there should be an agreement of all God's people in America, that are well affected to this work, to keep a day of fasting and prayer to God." This would be a concerted time where people would humble themselves, thank God for signs of his work, and beg him to pour out his Spirit upon his ministers, "that he would bow the heavens and come down, and erect his glorious kingdom through the earth." By believers' praying on the same day, the "union and agreement of God's people in his worship" would be more visible and known; such would "mightily encourage and animate God's saints," as well as "assist and enliven the devotions of Christians."[17]

Praying for Millennial Glory

It is possible that when Edwards suggested the idea of prayer unions, he was already familiar with those beginning in Scotland. By 1744, there was movement on both sides of the Atlantic to link Anglo-America together in united prayer for revival and reform. By the following year, Edwards had worked together with other ministers to establish a quarterly meeting for prayer in several towns and was eager to see this partnership extended. To that end, he published a lengthy argument for concerted prayer in 1747: *An Humble Attempt*.[18]

[16]Ibid., 4:519–20.
[17]Ibid., 4:520.
[18]Marsden, *Jonathan Edwards*, 333–40.

In *An Humble Attempt*, Edwards took prayer for revival and set it into a more cosmic, global framework. In the Bible, we have "the expressly revealed will of God, that his church should be very much in prayer for that glorious outpouring of the Spirit that is to be in the latter days, and the things that shall be accomplished by it." During these latter, millennial days, "every nation on the face of the whole earth shall be converted to Christianity, and every country shall be full of true Christians"; there will be more prosperity for the church in those days than in all the ages of history to that point; it will be a "time of general holiness" in which all heresies and false doctrines will be "exploded," and superstitious forms of worship "abolished." Far from merely private prayers for "the state of our own souls and the souls of our near neighbors," such concerted, extraordinary prayer is that "God may be glorified in the world" as his kingdom comes.[19]

The means that God will use to bring in this millennial glory is the prayer of God's people, united together to seek him. "There is no way that Christians in a private capacity can do so much to promote the work of God, and advance the kingdom of Christ, as by prayer." And this is especially the case when God's people are united to seek him. "Union," Edwards commented, "is one of the most amiable things, that pertains to human society; yea, 'tis one of the most beautiful and happy things on earth, which indeed makes earth most like heaven." As Christians, dispersed all over the world, are united to one another, they become "one holy society, one city, one family, one body" and so have a foretaste of that millennial joy for which they are praying. United prayer is beautiful, excellent, and reflective of God's own being.[20]

And there was great reason to hope that the time of God's latter day glory was drawing near. After all, the recently completed awakening was one sign of what God may do. In 1741,

---

[19] "An Humble Attempt," *WJE*, 5:348, 342, 343, 338, 339; Jonathan Edwards, "Importunate Prayer for Millennial Glory," in *WJE*, 22:375, 376.
[20] "Some Thoughts Concerning the Present Revival," *WJE*, 4:338–39, 518; "An Humble Attempt," *WJE*, 5:364–65.

Edwards certainly felt this was the case: "Now God seems in his providence, in an especial manner, to be calling us to be ready for those times. God seems to be as it were coming forth out of his place to do some extraordinary thing." This extraordinary thing was "so remarkable a pouring out of the Spirit of God in many places and the commotion the nations of the world seem to be in," signs that God was at work in bringing his work of redemption to new heights.[21]

The focus of the prayers of God's people should be the advancement of God's kingdom and the bringing in of his millennial glory. After all, Edwards reasoned, the model prayer, sometimes called "The Lord's Prayer," argues as much. The prayer begins with a petition that God's name be glorified, "which teaches us that we should be more concerned that God may be glorified in the world than our private interests promoted." And then, in praying for the coming of God's kingdom and for his will to be done on earth as it is in heaven, "we are directed to pray that God's kingdom may come, which has a special respect to the glorious estate of the church which is to be brought to pass in the latter days." Hence, over half of the petitions in the Lord's Prayer "do respect the state of God's church and the world of mankind: and those mentioned in the first place, before any of those petitions that respect our own selves and our own separate interests, which ought to be remembered and considered by all the professed followers and disciples of Christ."[22]

And this was how Edwards brought the local and global together in prayer. In many ways, he was the model of what he longed for among his people.

> I had great longings for the advancement of Christ's kingdom in the world. My secret prayer used to be in great part taken up in praying for it. If I heard the least hint of anything that happened in any part of the world, that appeared to me in some respect or other, to have a favorable aspect on the interest of

---

[21]"Importunate Prayer for Millennial Glory," *WJE*, 22:372
[22]Ibid., *WJE*, 22:376.

Christ's kingdom, my soul eagerly catched at it; and it would much animate and refresh me.

As his affections were stirred and warmed in delight for Christ, he longed for Christ's kingdom to advance; his soul sought for news about the increase of Christ's church; and his prayers moved beyond his private, selfish concerns to disinterested love for God's cause in the world. In many ways, prayer served not only as the voice of faith, but also as the discipline of disinterested benevolence.[23]

Yet, it was not always easy to pray for Christ's kingdom to come. When he was twenty-three years old, Edwards confided to his diary, "Have not in time past in my prayers, enough insisted upon the glorifying God in the world, and the advancement of the kingdom of Christ, the prosperity of the church, and the good of men." What he urged his people to do, Edwards had to urge for himself: entering into prayer with an eye to what God is doing in the world and a hope that the kingdom is coming.[24]

---

[23] "Personal Narrative," WJE, 16:797.
[24] Jonathan Edwards, "Diary," February 5, 1723/4, in WJE, 16:784.

CHAPTER 12

The Christian Life as a Journey to Heaven

In September 1733, Edwards first preached a sermon that became one of his favorites. Drawing from Hebrews 11:13–14, he pictured the Christian life as a journey or a pilgrimage toward heaven. This journey is "ascending" on a narrow pathway: "We must be content to travel up hill," he declared, "though it be hard, and tiresome, and contrary to the natural tendency and bias of our flesh." It is a journey that begins as early as possible in one's life and extends through death. Children can begin their journey to heaven. Edwards declared, "We ought to begin early. This should be the first concern and business that persons engage in when they come to be capable of acting, or doing any business." And this journey is to be pursued until death takes the Christian home to glory. "We ought to persevere in this way as long as we live. We should hold out in it to the end."[1]

---

[1]Jonathan Edwards, "The True Christian's Life a Journey Towards Heaven," in *The Works of Jonathan Edwards* (hereafter *WJE*), vol. 17, *Sermons and Discourses, 1730–1733*, ed.

Viewing the Christian life as a journey means that the believer should focus his or her heart on the end of the journey. One upshot of this is that this world is not the believer's home. "We ought not to rest in this world and its enjoyments, but should desire home," Edwards taught. "We should not be willing to have these things for our portion, but should seek happiness in another world." We should desire the journey's end. As every traveler understands, the ultimate goal of any journey is to get home. God never designed this world to be home; rather, "the future world was designed to be our settled and everlasting abode. . . . Heaven is that place alone where is to [be] obtained our highest end, and highest good."[2]

The reason heaven is our home, the place of our highest end and highest good, is that it is where God is, who is our highest good. When believers get to heaven, "there we shall be brought to a perfect union with God." There all sin will be fully and finally cleansed away and "we shall have the clear views of God's glory: we shall see face to face, and know as we are known." There believers will be comformed to God. "Then will our hearts be wholly a pure and holy offering to God, offered all in the flame of divine love." All the blessings of life in this world pale in comparison with the fully realized, seen, savored glory of God. "These are but shadows; but God is the substance. These are but scattered beams; but God is the sun. These are but streams; but God is the fountain. These are but drops; but God is the ocean."[3]

For those who understand this, who view the Christian life as a journey to their true home, death holds no terror. Though death wears "a fearful aspect," it is actually "a great blessing." While these saints live, they recognize they are on a journey and they long for the end of it in heaven: "Now they are got to heaven; they are got home; they never were at home before. They are got to their Father's house. They find more comfort, a thousand times,

Mark Valeri (New Haven, CT: Yale University Press, 1999), 431, 433, 434.
[2]Ibid., 17:430, 436, 437.
[3]Ibid., 17:437, 438.

now they are got home, than they did on their journey." In order to die well, the Christian must remember that he is exchanging sorrows for "exceeding joy" because he is arriving home.[4]

Edwards was certainly not unusual in viewing the Christian life as a journey to heaven. However, his ministry was characterized by a thorough and sustained focus on the ages and stages of the Christian life, a focus that was a bit unusual. From his privileging of the spirituality of childhood and early adulthood, to his exhortations and struggles with those who were "middle aged" and "old aged," he tried to pastor people individually and his church collectively through the stages of the Christian life. And his pastoral goal was that he might encourage each believer to arrive at heaven safely. As he urged his people:

> Let Christians help one another in going this journey. There are many ways that Christians might greatly help and forward one another in their way to heaven: by religious conference and otherwise. . . . This is the way to be more successful in traveling and to have the more joyful meeting at their Father's house in glory.[5]

Childhood

As historian Kenneth Minkema has pointed out, Edwards divided human life into four stages: childhood, youth, middle age, and old age. While childhood properly starts with infancy, Edwards focused on the stage beginning around six or seven years old and extending to around fifteen. He considered youth to extend from around fifteen to about twenty-five, and middle age from twenty-five to fifty years old, beyond which is old age. Throughout his ministry, Edwards focused on each age and stage and sought to heighten the affections of each age group.[6]

---

[4]Ibid., 17:438, 439.

[5]Ibid., 17:446. For a scholarly treatment that traces the theme of the Christian journey in Puritan piety, see Charles Hambrick-Stowe, *The Practice of Piety: Puritan Devotional Disciplines in Seventeenth-Century New England* (Chapel Hill: University of North Carolina Press, 1982).

[6]Kenneth P. Minkema, "Old Age and Religion in the Writings and Life of Jonathan Edwards," *Church History* 70 (2001): 680–82. See also Catherine A. Brekus, "Children

Edwards paid particular attention to children. Most famously, he used four-year-old Phebe Bartlet as an example of the awakening's converting power in his *Faithful Narrative*. Phebe was moved by the witness of another to engage in earnest prayer, desire to enjoy God, and long to serve him and gain an interest in him. She was concerned for her friends who did not know Christ and would weep because they were going to hell. She began strict observance of the Lord's Day, loved "to hear Mr. Edwards preach," and sought out religious conversation. All of this is familiar, but what many have missed is that Phebe was awakened through the witness of her eleven-year-old brother. One child led another child to love Christ.[7]

Citing Phebe as an example of genuine religious affections did not mean that Edwards viewed children as Christians by nature. He repeatedly taught that children are by nature sinful and deserving of God's wrath. "Infants are not looked upon by God as sinless, but that they are by nature children of wrath, seeing this terrible evil comes so heavily on mankind in infancy." Scripture represents all people "as being of a wicked heart from their youth, so in other places they are spoken of as being thus from the womb." Adam's sin has been imputed to infants, and so they are truly guilty and exposed to eternal punishment. No matter how innocent children may seem, "yet if they are out of Christ, they are not so in God's sight, but are young vipers, and are infinitely more hateful than vipers, and are in a most miserable condition."[8]

In order to awaken children to their lost condition and turn their hearts to Christ, Edwards held special meetings specifically geared to them. In one sermon preached to children in August

of Wrath, Children of Grace: Jonathan Edwards and the Puritan Culture of Child Rearing," in *The Child in Christian Thought*, ed. Marcia J. Burge (Grand Rapids: Eerdmans, 2001), 300–328.
[7]Jonathan Edwards, "A Faithful Narrative of the Surprising Work of God," in *WJE*, vol. 4, *The Great Awakening*, ed. C. C. Goen (New Haven, CT: Yale University Press, 1972), 199, 202.
[8]Jonathan Edwards, *WJE*, vol. 3, *Original Sin*, ed. Clyde A. Holbrook (New Haven, CT: Yale University Press, 1970), 215–16, 266, 410–12; Jonathan Edwards, "Some Thoughts Concerning the Present Revival of Religion (1742)," in *WJE*, 4:394.

1740, he argued that "children ought to love the Lord Jesus Christ above all things in this world." In particular, children should love Jesus even more than they love their parents. In arguing for this, Edwards noted that Jesus is lovelier than any other being and is full of mercy and holiness. "Yea, he is so lovely a person, that God the Father infinitely delights in him; he is his beloved Son, the brightness of his glory, whose beauty God continually sees with infinite delight, without ever being weary of beholding it," Edwards said. Because Jesus is lovelier, there is more good to enjoy in him. Jesus is the bread of life; he offers glorious clothing and ornaments; his spiritual good is like gold and tastes as good as honey. He has a right to children, both because he made them and because he suffered for them. There is none like him.[9]

While Edwards appealed to children by means of the glories of Christ, he also motivated them by pointing up the terrors that would result from not loving Jesus. "All children are by nature children of wrath and are in danger of eternal damnation in hell," Edwards forthrightly told them. Up to that point, Christ had protected them from death and the grave where "they would have been eaten up of worms long ago"; from the Devil, who would "immediately fall upon and carry them away" if Christ permitted; from damnation, in which "they would have been burning in hell among devils long before this time"; and in their sleep. What children need to recognize is "how angry God is with [them]" that they do not love Christ. Edwards warned them, "If you don't love Christ, you are under God's curse, and if you never love him, will be a cursed miserable creature forever." Even more, "you deserve that he should hate you all the days of your life, and that he should cast you into hell forever."[10]

The hope for children, as for the rest of humankind, is to run to Jesus and to seek conversion. Children need the blood of Christ, Edwards told them, "to cleanse you from this guilt of your not

[9]Jonathan Edwards, "Children Ought to Love the Lord Jesus Christ Above All," in *WJE*, vol. 22, *Sermons and Discourses, 1739–1742*, ed. Harry S. Stout, Nathan O. Hatch, with Kyle Farley (New Haven, CT: Yale University Press, 2003), 171, 172.
[10]Ibid., 22:174, 176.

loving Christ and all your disobedience to him." If they would trust Jesus, they would discover that "God would fill their hearts with love to Christ now while they are young." Such a "holy principle of love to Christ in your hearts" would make children fit to live in this world and fit to die. And if they do die in their childhood, as so many did in eighteenth-century New England, their faith would be a comfort to their parents; if they survive childhood, their faith would be a comfort to themselves. "It is sweet to the soul to love Christ. It is an holy affection that fills the soul with sweetness. And then you will have the pleasure of living a life of communion with Christ, which will be a very sweet life."[11]

Such sermons were not unusual either for Edwards or for his fellow New England ministers. And they were extremely successful. After the awakening came to a close in 1742, Edwards reported to a fellow minister that during that time "we had the most wonderful work among children that ever was in Northampton. The former great outpouring of the Spirit was remarkable for influences upon the minds of children, beyond all that had ever been before; but this far exceeded that." Such success in preaching to children led Edwards to continue the practice throughout the awakening.[12]

Some critics of the awakening suggested that preaching to "poor innocent children" about "hell fire and eternal damnation" was inappropriate. Edwards would have none of their objections.

> Why should we conceal the truth from them? Will those children that have been dealt tenderly with in this respect, and lived and died insensible of their misery till they come to feel it in hell, ever thank parents and others for their tenderness, in not letting them know what they were in danger of?

In the end, success was its own argument: "I have seen the happy effects of dealing plainly and thoroughly with children in the

---

[11]Ibid., 22:177, 178, 179.
[12]Jonathan Edwards to Thomas Prince, December 12, 1743, in *WJE*, vol. 16, *Letters and Personal Writings*, ed. George S. Claghorn (New Haven, CT: Yale University Press, 1998), 119.

concerns of their souls, without sparing them at all, in many instances; and never knew any ill consequence of it, in any one instance." If children can begin the Christian journey early in life, so much the better for them and for the cause of Christ.[13]

Youth

While Edwards focused on children, he banked his ministry on reaching the "youth" of the town. He was concerned that as children get older and more used to sin and sinning, they become harder to convert. In an early sermon, he observed that "man, when he first comes into the world, is like a young twig, easily bent; but the longer you suffer yourself to grow at random, the more you will be like an inflexible tree: your heart hardens so fast, that you will find the work of religion much more difficult the longer delayed." It is absolutely vital that men and women are converted before the concerns of adulthood overwhelm their spiritual senses.[14]

Not only was there a pastoral motivation for his focus on youth, but there was also a demographic one. As historian Patricia Tracy demonstrated in great detail, the youth of Northampton were marrying later, securing their own land or starting their own businesses later, and so entering into the world of adulthood with its responsibilities later than previous generations. Many of the "youthful sins" that Edwards decried were the result of what we would now call "prolonged adolescence," as young men and women found themselves with too much time on their hands and too little sense of direction for their lives. By focusing on "young people," Edwards not only sought to control a socially diverse demographic bloc in his community; he also attempted to provide this generation with a way to channel its longings and desires in the only way where they would be fully

---

[13]"Some Thoughts Concerning the Present Revival," *WJE*, 4:394. See also pp. 407–8, where Edwards defends separate meetings for children.

[14]Jonathan Edwards, "The Duty of Hearkening to God's Voice," in *WJE*, vol. 10, *Sermons and Discourses, 1720–1723*, ed. Wilson H. Kimnach (New Haven, CT: Yale University Press, 1992), 446–47.

and finally satisfied: by resting and receiving Christ alone and learning to delight in him.[15]

There was little doubt that Edwards felt that the young people of Northampton were falling prey to a number of sins that would destroy them. In his *Faithful Narrative*, published in 1737, he claimed that eight or nine years before,

> it seemed to be a time of extraordinary dullness in religion: licentiousness for some years greatly prevailed among the youth of the town; they were many of them very much addicted to night-walking, and frequenting the tavern, and lewd practices, wherein some, by their example exceedingly corrupted others.

Moreover, the young people would engage in "frolics," which brought young men and women together outside family oversight till all hours of the night.[16]

In 1748, Edwards was even more explicit about the sins of youth. During the funeral sermon for his daughter, Jerusha, he castigated the young people for their "customs" and "liberties" that were "of an evil and corrupt tendency":

> As, for instance, not only the gross acts of lasciviousness, but {also} such liberties as naturally tend to stir up lust: that shameful lascivious custom of handling women's breasts, and the different sexes lying in beds together—the custom of frolicking, as it is called; [and] of the so general custom of being absent from family prayer and being out very late in the night, and those of different sexes sitting up greater part of the night together.

Clearly sexual sins, ones that lead to "unclean imaginations {and} frequent lustful desires," were a major problem for Northampton youth.[17]

Edwards was concerned about the youths' "corrupt conversations" as well. He devoted an entire 1741 sermon to the topic in

---

[15]Patricia J. Tracy, *Jonathan Edwards, Pastor: Religion and Society in Eighteenth-Century Northampton* (New York: Hill and Wang, 1978), 99–106.
[16]"Faithful Narrative," *WJE*, 4:146.
[17]Jonathan Edwards, "Youth Is Like a Flower That Is Cut Down," in *WJE*, 22:333.

a meeting designed for the youth between the ages of fifteen and twenty-five. As he met with them, he urged the young people to "avoid all profane conversation," whether talking about sacred matters in a light or frivolous way or engaging in "unclean or lascivious communication." He arraigned some among their number as "foul-mouthed persons" who "seem to delight in unclean songs and telling lascivious stories, and in talking with a bold air of those things that modesty forbids to mention, and seem to look upon as their honor that they dare break over rules of modesty in their talk, as if it was a great attainment." Even if some did not engage in such talk, they appeared to applaud the filthy-mouthed: "With many young people, he is the best man, that shows most of that kind of wit and boldness that appears in lascivious jesting." Sexual activity and dirty talk were chief among the problems that Edwards discerned.[18]

In response, Edwards's preaching to the young people sought to demonstrate that now is the time to seek salvation. In one early sermon to Northampton youth, from Ecclesiastes 12:1, he urged that "the time of youth is the best time to be improved to religious purposes." Not only do young people have more opportunity to spend their time seeking godliness, but they also will discover that it is the time when they are most susceptible to spiritual influences. Awakening sermons and "awakening providences" are more apt to seize the attention of young people and be used for spiritual good. Above all, youth is the likeliest time when one will have God's assistance and blessing in seeking salvation.[19]

Even more important was how Edwards sought to allure his young people with the thought that piety brings pleasures superior to those offered by the world. One of Edwards's most repreached sermons was written in May 1734 on the theme, "Youth and the Pleasures of Piety." In it, he argued that while young people are notable for their pursuit of pleasure, the plea-

---

[18]Jonathan Edwards, "The Danger of Corrupt Communication among Young People," in *WJE*, 22:159, 160.
[19]Jonathan Edwards, "Sermon on Eccl. 12:1(a)," in *WJE Online*, vol. 46, *Sermons, Series II, 1731–1732* (Jonathan Edwards Center at Yale University, 2008), L. 2v.

sures of the world and the flesh pale in comparison with those offered by Christ. "Hereby they may obtain pleasures that are of a more noble and excellent kind," he observed. "Hereby may be obtained pleasures that are more solid and substantial," ones that are "vastly sweeter, and more exquisitely delighting, and are of a more satisfying nature." Pleasures of beauty, love and friendship, gratification of appetite, pleasant company: all are found by following Christ and delighting in him. Young people may believe that their illicit sexual activity and talk is pleasurable, but that is nothing compared with the love of Christ.

> There is a most dear friendship between him and them. Their souls are espoused to Christ, their hearts are knit to him, and their love has an infinitely more beautiful and lovely object than that of earthly lovers. Their love is not despised, but accepted of Christ: they may freely have access to Christ at all times to express their love.

Here is pleasure that is rich, satisfying, and delightful.[20]

Far better than the profane and lewd conversations in which they were engaged, piety would make their company keeping and other innocent pleasures sweeter. "It is a strange notion that many young people have, that company will be the worse for being virtuous," Edwards commented. But vice, whether in word or deed, provides no real benefit. "Young people do the devil all that service gratis. They get nothing by it for the present: they undo themselves, without so much as getting any present pleasure by it."[21]

In order to know these pleasures, young people must close with Christ. "Seek that divine grace in your heart, whereby your soul may be beautified, and adorned, and rendered lovely in the eyes of God; and whereby you may live a life of divine love, a life of love to Christ, and communion with him." In doing so,

---

[20]Jonathan Edwards, "Youth and the Pleasures of Piety," in *WJE*, vol. 19, *Sermons and Discourses, 1734–1738*, ed. M. X. Lesser (New Haven, CT: Yale University Press, 2001), 82, 83, 84.
[21]Ibid., 19:86–87.

young people will develop "spiritual and heavenly appetites" that are "fitted for those noble and excellent pleasures which you have now heard."[22]

For a time, it appeared that the young people heeded Edwards. In one 1738 sermon, he directed a word to the young people, noting how they had left off "those disorders" such as "frequenting the tavern; to night-walking, and frolicking, and rioting, and licentious company-keeping." And he begged them, "Don't return to any disorders, and licentious practices, or anything that is not of good report. Show yourselves ready to hearken to come and set as you have done, that you may be a generation to God's praise." By the time he left Northampton in 1750, he was not sure whether they had actually heeded him or not. Still, he could truthfully say in his valedictory sermon, "Since I have been settled in the work of the ministry in this place, I have ever had a peculiar concern for the souls of the young people, and a desire that religion might flourish among them; and have especially exerted myself in order to it."[23]

Middle Age and Old Age

Compared with the amount of time spent on children, Edwards focused relatively little on those older than twenty-five, and much of what he said was negative. This was the generation that had come of age during the ministry of his predecessor and grandfather, Solomon Stoddard. As such, they were largely resistant to Edwards's leadership during the Great Awakening as a whole and especially the "Qualifications Controversy" that dominated the last three years of his ministry.[24]

---

[22]Ibid., 19:89.

[23]Jonathan Edwards, "A City on a Hill," in *WJE*, 19:558; Jonathan Edwards, "A Farewell Sermon," in *WJE*, vol. 25, *Sermons and Discourses, 1743–1758*, ed. Wilson H. Kimnach (New Haven, CT: Yale University Press 2006), 482. As Edwards noted in his farewell sermon, part of what went wrong in his ministry to the young people was the "Bad Book Episode": see George M. Marsden, *Jonathan Edwards: A Life* (New Haven, CT: Yale University Press, 2003), 292–302, and Ava Chamberlain, "Bad Books and Bad Boys: The Transformation of Gender in Eighteenth-Century Northampton, Massachusetts," in *Jonathan Edwards at Home and Abroad: Historical Memories, Cultural Movements, Global Horizons*, ed. David W. Kling and Douglas A. Sweeney (Columbia: University of South Carolina Press, 2003), 61–81.

[24]On this, see especially Tracy, *Jonathan Edwards, Pastor*, and Minkema, "Old Age and Religion."

Of course, one can easily recognize that Edwards directed most of his ministry to the "adults," the middle-aged and older people who made up his congregation. But he also preached specific sermons to those who would be leaders within his congregation and town, urging them to press on in their discipleship. Particularly, he urged those who headed households to use their influence to further the awakening. During the heightened time of awakening, in 1741, Edwards gave a sermon in a private meeting for the "middle aged" in which he argued that "after a dead time in religion, 'tis very requisite that religion should revive in heads of families and those that have the care of children, in order to a people's being fitted for so great a privilege as to have God remarkably dwelling among them." As he reflected on what happened during the previous revival period—especially the declension that came after 1735—Edwards identified what had happened: the middle aged and elderly had turned from renewed Christianity to their favorite sins. After all, "the sins of such as have greatest public influences are most regarded of God in his public dealings," Edwards said. "God is chiefly provoked with the town by sins of elderly people." Some of those sins included coldness and dullness in religion and "corrupt frames," which could only hinder the awakening of children and youth.[25]

The only appropriate response of this generation was to "seek that your hearts may be now broken that you have lived so long and lived no better." If the middle aged would seek the Lord, it would bring about a permanent state of renewing. Not only this, but parents should "be very assiduous in instructing the principal means of grace" and "never let [children] rest till you can see 'em awakened." Further, parents should insist on "strict government," that is, they should not let their children and youths wander the streets at night, carousing, frolicking, and bundling. Above all, earnest prayer was necessary. "You should travail for them," Edwards counseled.[26]

---

[25]Jonathan Edwards, "The Importance of Revival Among Heads of Families," in *WJE*, 22:451, 452, 453.
[26]Ibid., 22:453, 454.

A few years later, Edwards offered the same instructions to the middle aged in his congregation. In a 1748 lecture on Ephesians 6:4, Edwards placed upon parents the burden of teaching children the truth of the Christian faith. Parents are not only to teach their children about Christ and their duty to him, but they are also to assist them in distinguishing "the nature of true religion" from counterfeits. Parents should restrain children from sinning and lead them by example to paths of holiness. Such education—positive and negative—should begin with infancy and continue throughout the child-rearing cycle. Part of the motivation comes from recognizing the tremendous responsibility parents have: children look to them for spiritual as well as natural care. The Devil himself seeks their destruction from the time they enter the world. More motivation comes from understanding what actually happens in infant baptism. At that time, the parents "did professedly give 'em up; that implied that you would if you had opportunity treat them accordingly, and that is use them as God's, as those you had devoted to him and so bring 'em up for him and practically give 'em to God." Edwards urged parents to make sure that the children have the necessary schools, where they might be instructed in the precepts of Christianity, but especially that their own "precept and example" might serve to train their children in godliness.[27]

While Edwards was able to give the middle aged specific instructions about how they could be useful in their Christian journey, he seemed to have little to say to "aged men and women." While he urged them to seek Christ, he wondered "what is the reason you han't revivals as well as young converts." Among the reasons he suggested were "long slothfulness," covetousness, pride and selfishness, "family sins," and contention. Part of his negativity came from his view of sin. As sinful dispositions are inclined toward sin in such a way that long-formed habits dominate, it is much less likely that change will occur. As he put it in one sermon, "If [it] were only that you are growing older,

---

[27]Jonathan Edwards, "Sermon on Eph. 6:4," in *WJE Online*, vol. 66, *Sermons, Series II, 1748* (Jonathan Edwards Center at Yale University, 2008), L. 2r., L. 6v., L. 13v. col. 2.

there would be less likelihood of your being awakened again, for as persons grow older they grow less and less susceptive of convictions. Evil habits grow stronger and more deeply rooted in the heart."[28]

That did not mean that Edwards was hopeless about the aged. He continued to exhort them to follow Christ. For example, in one sermon preached in 1735 during the height of the early awakening, he declared, "Now there seems to be a door opened for old sinners. . . . Though [you are] old in sin, God has put a new and extraordinary advantage into your hands." Though the aged may lament that they have not followed Christ sincerely from their youth, now is a final opportunity to be converted. And by his testimony, many were. Both in the earlier awakening and the later one (1739–1742), Edwards saw conversions among the middle aged and elderly. But on the whole, his verdict was that God had "cast off the old and stiff-necked generation." That would not bode well for his long-term service as Northampton's minister.[29]

Dying Well

The end of the Christian journey is death, whether for those in infancy or for the elderly. One of Edwards's pastoral preoccupations was helping his people die well. And he used funeral sermons as a means to instruct those of every age to prepare for the end of this life and the beginning of the next. By looking at two such sermons preached for those closest to him—his grandmother Esther Stoddard and his disciple and model of piety David Brainerd—we may recognize how Edwards viewed the end of the Christian journey.

In his 1736 funeral sermon for his grandmother, Edwards drew upon Revelation 14:13 to picture both what the Christian life is like and in what the Christian hope consists. The believer's life is one of good works. "The saints han't only a holy heart,

---

[28] Jonathan Edwards, "Aged Men and Women Joyfully Receiving Christ," in *WJE*, 22:459–60; Jonathan Edwards, "God Makes Men Sensible of Their Misery Before He Reveals His Mercy and Love," in *WJE*, 17:168.
[29] Jonathan Edwards, "Pressing into the Kingdom," in *WJE*, 19:301; "Faithful Narrative," *WJE*, 4:158; "Some Thoughts," *WJE*, 4:506.

but do live a holy life. The tree is not only good, and the root good, but the fruit is good." Genuine saints have a faith that is alive and active in good works. But the Christian hope is that

> when the life of a saint is at an end and they depart into another world, their works do follow them. While they live, they live a life of good works, and when they come to die and their life ceases yet their good works don't leave them but follow them into the eternal world where they go. There they shall reap the sweet fruit of them.

God keeps a book of remembrance that enables him to recall the good works of the saints for their blessing and everlasting reward.[30]

Such a life of good works entitles the believer to a great degree of glory in heaven.

> There are different degrees of glory in heaven. If the good works of the saints are rewarded in heaven, it will inevitably follow that there are different degrees of glory, for if a saint, when he does a good work, shall have no higher degree of happiness or glory in heaven than if he had not done it, then he has no reward for it. For in what sense can a person be said to be rewarded in heaven for such a good work which he has done when he has [no more glory or happiness] at all than if he had not done it.

Such should motivate believers to good works so that when they die, they will know more glory and more delight.[31]

By contrast, when Edwards preached Brainerd's funeral sermon in 1747, his focus moved from the rewards granted to our works to the glories enjoyed in the presence of the triune God. When saints are absent from the body, "they go to dwell in the immediate, full and constant sight or view" of Christ. Their sight is the promised "beatifical vision of God [which] is in Christ, who is that brightness of effulgence of God's glory." God's own light,

---

[30]Jonathan Edwards, "Sermon on Rev. 14:13(b)," in *WJE Online*, vol. 51, Sermons, Series II, 1736 (Jonathan Edwards Center at Yale University, 2008), L. 3r., L. 4v.
[31]Ibid., L. 9v.

mediated by Jesus, will fill heaven as men and women behold his glory. "They see the glory of his divine nature, consisting in all the glory of the Godhead, the beauty of all his perfections," Edwards declared. Even more, "they behold the marvelous glory of that work of his, the work of redemption, and of the glorious way of salvation by him," and they learn "what is the breadth and length and depth and height of the grace and love of Christ, appearing in his redemption." In heaven,

> they shall eat and drink abundantly, and swim in the ocean of love, and be eternally swallowed up in the infinitely bright, and infinitely mild and sweet beams of divine love; eternally receiving that light, eternally full of it, and eternally compassed round with it, and everlasting reflecting it back again to the fountain of it.[32]

But the other great advantage the saints in heaven will have is that they will be able to watch the continued progress of the work of redemption. As Christ enjoys and delights in the advance of the gospel, "undoubtedly the saints in heaven are partakers with Christ in the joy and glory of the advancement and prosperity of his kingdom of grace on earth, and success of the gospel here." In fact, the saints will be able to have "a full view of the state of the church on earth, and a speedy, direct and certain acquaintance with all its affairs, in every part." The shadows of this life fade away as the saints dwell in the clearest light and enjoy such great happiness.

> The happiness of the saints in heaven consists very much in beholding the glory of God appearing in the work of redemption: for 'tis by this that God manifests his glory. . . . And therefore undoubtedly their happiness consists very much in beholding the progress of this work, in its application and success, and the steps by which infinite power and wisdom brings it to its consummation.

---

[32]Jonathan Edwards, "True Saints, When Absent from the Body, Are Present with the Lord," in *WJE*, 25:229, 230, 233.

To die well is to have longed to delight in God's glory and to have prayed for God's kingdom because in heaven those longings will be satisfied eternally.[33]

Of course, these two messages were complementary for Edwards. Heaven, that world of love, will know degrees of bliss, but everyone will be so filled with delight in God's glory that all will redound to his praise. And in many ways, this is the place where the large picture of redemptive history and the more personal application of redemption merge. The great hope and expectation that Edwards had was that earth will be drawn up into heaven and all creation will join in heaven's music in praise to the triune God. "And thus they will live and thus they will reign in love, and in that godlike joy which is the blessed fruit of it, such as eye hath not seen, nor ear heard, nor hath ever entered into the heart of any in this world to conceive. And thus they will live and reign forever and ever." Such, after all, is God's grand design.[34]

[33]Ibid., 25:237, 238.
[34]Jonathan Edwards, "Charity and Its Fruits," in *WJE*, vol. 8, *Ethical Writings*, ed. Paul Ramsey (New Haven, CT: Yale University Press, 1989), 386.

"Where Do I Begin?"

An Annotated Bibliography

One of the things that makes the study of Jonathan Edwards overwhelming is the sheer amount of literature. First, of course, is the amount of material written by Edwards himself. While the definitive Yale University Press print edition filled twenty-six volumes, the Jonathan Edwards Center at Yale University has made available transcriptions of a wide range of materials online that total seventy-three "volumes." Obviously, any attempt to master Edwards is futile, although we now have a better opportunity and access than ever before to know what he said.

Also overwhelming is the vast expanse of secondary literature. M. X. Lesser, in his updated bibliography of Edwardsiana stretching over 276 years, totaled over six hundred pages with thousands of entries. Just from 1994 to 2005, he provided seven hundred entries of books, articles, and dissertations: that's seventy items per year on Edwards. I had a little experience with this, providing a bibliographical essay at the end of a book that I coedited with D. G. Hart and Stephen J. Nichols. That essay went nearly twenty pages, with over one hundred different items cited. And so, just as obviously, any attempt to master the secondary literature about Edwards is equally futile.[1]

But Edwards is worth the effort. Working through both primary and secondary sources will not only enrich one's understanding of the Christian life, but also inform one's perspective about life in Christ's church. All historical work is necessarily cross-cultural; people have to cross the boundaries of our time, place, and norms in order to understand another time, place, and set of norms well. And in doing this cross-cultural work, we gain a better appreciation not only of a past time, but also of our own.

So, to assist those who are interested in reading Edwards, I have prepared an annotated bibliography. It is important to say, as a preface to it, that these annotations represent my opinion. Imagine us walking through a bookstore together; I'm pulling books off the shelf and telling you my "take" on them. There are other "takes," and you need to listen to them as well. Those opinions can be discovered in academic reviews and more popular magazines, like *Books and Culture* or *Christianity Today*. With that preface, where shall we begin?

Biography

Before we dive into primary sources—the material written by Edwards himself—I think it is important to have context. The best way to gain context on Edwards is to work through a biography about him. There are several from which to choose.

---

[1]M. X. Lesser, *Reading Jonathan Edwards: An Annotated Bibliography in Three Parts, 1729–2005* (Grand Rapids: Eerdmans, 2008); Sean Michael Lucas, "Jonathan Edwards between Church and Academy: A Bibliographic Essay," in *The Legacy of Jonathan Edwards: American Religion and the Evangelical Tradition*, ed. D. G. Hart, Sean Michael Lucas, and Stephen J. Nichols (Grand Rapids: Baker, 2003), 228–47.

Marsden, George M. *Jonathan Edwards: A Life*. New Haven, CT: Yale University Press, 2003.

This is the best "big" biography of Edwards. One friend of mine called it encyclopedic. Taking full advantage of the Yale edition of Edwards as well as the best of scholarly insight, Marsden has crafted a biography that has been widely hailed. He started with the basic understanding that Edwards's central, organizing principle was the sovereignty of God and that his prime motivating principle was one's eternal relationship with such a Deity. Working from these points, Marsden more successfully locates Edwards in his times than any previous biographer. Edwards emerges as a quintessential Puritan theologian, an introverted New England pastor, and a thoughtful Reformed philosophical theologian.

Marsden, George M. *A Short Life of Jonathan Edwards*. Grand Rapids: Eerdmans, 2008.

Not content to write the best comprehensive biography, Marsden also has written the best "short life" of Edwards. But this book is not simply a condensation of his larger work. It is a fresh retelling, focusing on key episodes, important parallels (Marsden opens with a wonderful parallel between Edwards and Benjamin Franklin), and salient texts. Marsden's writing, always clear and crisp, is even more accessible; the book appears in Eerdmans's Library of Religious Biography, which books are useful for high school and college students, as well as general readers. Highly recommended for those who want an easy entry point to contextualizing Edwards.

Gura, Philip F. *Jonathan Edwards: America's Evangelical*. New York: Hill and Wang, 2005.

I thoroughly enjoyed this book when it was published and even used it in a class I taught on Edwards before the Marsden short biography became available. Its strengths are many: it is well-written and well-argued, and Gura helpfully locates Edwards's significance in the way he talked about "spiritual experience." According to Gura, Edwards provided "people new ways to approach their spirituality in their everyday lives, a practice based in a subjective, intuitive interpretation of religious experience" (90). Gura also usefully mines the developing historical understanding of colonial print culture and how it impacted Edwards's view of his ministry and colonials' view of the Great Awakening. This is a very valuable brief book.

That said, there are differences between Gura's telling and Marsden's epic tale. Perhaps one could put the difference this way—Gura's work embodies an old Harvard telling, whereas Marsden's represents a new Yale telling. Throughout his biography—all the way through to the acknowledgments—Gura replicates a number of the positions of Perry Miller and Alan Heimert, the two doyens of American literature at Harvard University from the 1940s through the 1980s, who did so much to revitalize the study of American Puritanism. His emphases on "the new sense" and "religious psychology," John Locke's and John Newton's influence on Edwards, and the importance of the jeremiad all represent the influence of Miller and Heimert. Reading Gura, one gets the sense that a number of the groundbreaking studies of Edwards that have come since the mid-1980s never were published (particularly, the recent emphases on Edwards's dispositional ontology, Trinitarian theology, and his engagement with deism). One is time-warped back to the state of affairs in Edwards studies when his Harvard mentors ruled the field.[2]

By contrast, Marsden's biography fully takes advantage of the tremendous amount of work done by those younger scholars associated with the Yale University *Works of Jonathan Edwards*

---

[2]The classic Perry Miller contributions were *Jonathan Edwards* (1949; repr., Amherst: University of Massachusetts Press, 1981); *The New England Mind: The Seventeenth Century* (1939; repr., Cambridge: Harvard University Press, 1983); *The New England Mind: From Colony to Province* (1953; repr., Cambridge: Harvard University Press, 1983); and *Errand into the Wilderness* (Cambridge: Harvard University Press, 1956). The great Alan Heimert book was *Religion and the American Mind: From the Great Awakening to the Revolution* (Cambridge: Harvard University Press, 1966).

project. In addition, Marsden, as well as a number of the Yale scholars led by Harry Stout, is an evangelical, which colors his approach with a more appreciative and sure-footed theological cast. In particular, he places Edwards's continuing importance in exactly the right place: it was Edwards's all-encompassing vision of God's glorious sovereignty over all things, not the way he empowered human agency through the religion of the heart, that ultimately explained historically his cultural staying power and continuing influence. And perhaps this is the place where Marsden's and Gura's views of Edwards most clearly part ways— Marsden, in line with the evangelicals helping to lead the Yale *Works of Jonathan Edwards*, is quite comfortable with Edwards's Calvinist theological vision, while Gura, like his Harvard mentors, found Edwards's relevance in his being the voice of (post) modern spirituality.

Murray, Iain H. *Jonathan Edwards: A New Biography*. Carlisle, PA: Banner of Truth, 1987.

Though over twenty years old, this biography still has value, especially in its forthright appreciation of Edwards's Calvinism and approach to revival. Though Murray seems not to have fully appreciated the work of the Jonathan Edwards Center at Yale University, the editors of Edwards's works, his love for Edwards is undeniable. For those looking for a heroic biography, this would be the book to read.

Edwards on the Christian Life

It would be incredibly unhelpful for me simply to tell someone to read everything Edwards wrote. And so, I will give you the same advice that D. Martyn Lloyd-Jones gave: "Revivals have often started as a result of people reading volumes such as these two volumes of Edwards' works. So read this man. Decide to do so. Read his sermons; read his practical treatises, and then go on to the great discourses on theological topics." That's good advice and what I would urge for anyone beginning to read Edwards for benefit in his or her Christian life.[3]

Edwards, Jonathan. *The Sermons of Jonathan Edwards: A Reader*, ed. Wilson H. Kimnach, Kenneth P. Minkema, and Douglas A. Sweeney. New Haven, CT: Yale University Press, 1999.

This is the finest collection of Edwards's sermons. Not only do the editors include all the important sermons—"Sinners in the Hands of an Angry God," "God Glorified in Man's Redemption," "A Divine and Supernatural Light," "Heaven Is a World of Love"—but their principle of arrangement is excellent:

> The sermons have been arranged to reflect the various stages in a hypothetical cycle of preaching addressing various spiritual conditions assumed by Edwards' religious culture, from an introduction to religious experience through various levels of instruction and discipline to the ultimate vision of the soul in heaven. (xvi)

Edwards, Jonathan. *Jonathan Edwards's Sinners in the Hands of an Angry God: A Casebook*, ed. Wilson H. Kimnach, Caleb J. D. Maskell, and Kenneth P. Minkema. New Haven, CT: Yale University Press, 2010.

This extremely valuable little book focuses on Edwards's most famous sermon. Not only do the editors provide historical and theological background for understanding the sermon, as well as the sermon itself, but they also have collected a wide range of secondary sources for interpretation. Readers can compare "Sinners" with Gilbert Tennent's famous sermon "The Dangers of an Unconverted Ministry," read Harriet Beecher Stowe's reflections

---

[3]D. Martyn Lloyd-Jones, "Jonathan Edwards and the Crucial Importance of Revival," in *The Puritans: Their Origins and Successors* (Carlisle, PA: Banner of Truth, 1987), 369–70. The two volumes of Edwards's works to which Lloyd-Jones refers are Jonathan Edwards, *The Works of Jonathan Edwards*, ed. Edward Hickman, 2 vols. (1834; repr., Carlisle, PA: Banner of Truth, 1974).

on Edwardsian theology in *The Minister's Wooing*, and consider the place of Edwards's theology in the light of the late twentieth-century "Toronto Blessing." Fascinating.

Edwards, Jonathan. *A Jonathan Edwards Reader*, ed. John E. Smith, Harry S. Stout, and Kenneth P. Minkema. New Haven, CT: Yale University Press, 1995.

For those unsure that they want to tackle a full-length Edwards treatise, this reader provides an excellent sampling of Edwards's writings. Here one will find material drawn from the wide range of the Edwardsian corpus: "Images of Divine Things," *A Faithful Narrative*, "A History of the Work of Redemption," personal writings, and important letters. In addition, there are significant selections from the main treatises: *Religious Affections*; *An Humble Inquiry*; *Freedom of the Will*; *Original Sin*; and *The Nature of True Virtue*.

Edwards, Jonathan. *The Works of Jonathan Edwards*, vol. 2, *Religious Affections*, ed. John E. Smith. New Haven, CT: Yale University Press, 1959.

If we follow Lloyd-Jones's advice to move from sermons to practical treatises, this is the Edwardsian treatise to read. In this book, two chapters were devoted to themes from *Religious Affections*, but I would suggest that this treatise was foundational for everything that Edwards thought and wrote about the Christian life. No less a historian than Perry Miller called *Religious Affections* "the most profound exploration of the religious psychology in all American literature." And now that this edition of the treatise is available in paperback from Yale University Press for little more than the cost of a bag of good coffee at Starbucks, there is really little excuse for not reading it. For those who are still afraid of the book, a good alternative might be Sam Storms, *Signs of the Spirit: An Interpretation of Jonathan Edwards's "Religious Affections"* (Wheaton, IL: Crossway, 2007).[4]

---

[4]Miller, *Jonathan Edwards*, 177.

Edwards, Jonathan. *The Works of Jonathan Edwards*, vol. 9, *A History of the Work of Redemption*, ed. John F. Wilson. New Haven, CT: Yale University Press, 1989.

My hope is that you have been convinced of the importance of this sermon series for Edwards's understanding of God's grand design and its significance for the Christian life. Edwards never had the opportunity to revise and publish these sermons, but that did not stop his literary executors from doing so in 1774. The series was first edited by Edwards's Scottish correspondent John Erskine, and it appears that considerable liberties were taken with the text. For those interested in what Edwards actually preached, the Yale edition went back to the original sermon manuscripts for a new transcription. While this has not yet been made available in paperback, the introduction written by editor John Wilson is nearly worth the price for the hardback.

Edwards, Jonathan. *The Works of Jonathan Edwards*, vol. 8, *Ethical Writings*, ed. Paul Ramsey. New Haven, CT: Yale University Press, 1989.

Though originally slated to be edited by H. Richard Niebuhr, the great Yale ethicist, this project fell to Paul Ramsey shortly before his death. The volume brings together three of Edwards's most significant writings, all of which were published posthumously: *Charity and Its Fruits*, *The End for Which God Created the World*, and *The Nature of True Virtue*. Ramsey demonstrates the liberties that Edwards's previous editors took with these manuscripts. In several instances, the editorial practices significantly shifted Edwards's meaning. Reading these texts in this version not only puts one back to the "real" Edwards; it also is a profoundly enriching spiritual experience.

For those who want to read Edwards's essay *The End for Which God Created the World* in a more accessible form, John Piper's *God's Passion for His Glory: Living the Vision of Jonathan Edwards* (Wheaton, IL: Crossway, 1998) is extremely valuable. It includes not only Edwards's text, but also a personal, biographical explanation of Edwards's significance in the life of an important evangelical minister today. Not to be missed.

Edwards, Jonathan. *The Works of Jonathan Edwards*, vol. 4, *The Great Awakening*, ed. C. C. Goen. New Haven, CT: Yale University Press, 1972.

This is another key Edwardsian text now available in paperback. As I have tried to demonstrate, the texts contained in *The Great Awakening* are key for understanding how the Christian life develops in the cauldron of revival and renewal: *A Faithful Narrative*; *Distinguishing Marks of the Work of the Spirit of God*; *Some Thoughts on the Present Revival of Religion*. Goen's introduction helpfully situates these texts in the larger context of the Great Awakening. The book also continues the various versions of *A Faithful Narrative*, from the first letter written by Edwards in 1735 to the final Boston version of 1738.

Those who might be interested in reading Edwards's *Distinguishing Marks*, his 1741 sermon on the Great Awakening, in a modernized form, with commentary, may want to check out R. C. Sproul and Archie Parrish, *The Spirit of Revival: Discovering the Wisdom of Jonathan Edwards* (Wheaton, IL: Crossway, 2000).

Now, they say that confession is good for the soul, so here is mine: I am not a huge fan of Edwards's more philosophical treatises. You may have noticed that there is a major gap in this book; there is not a significant direct reference to Edwards's *Freedom of the Will*. Part of the reason is that it is difficult to understand. Another part is that it does not strike me as very relevant to the Christian life. I know that others would disagree with me, but there it is. The only other volume in the Yale edition that was not directly referenced in the text of this book was *The Life of David Brainerd*. I am not a big fan of that book either. While Edwards attempted to produce a case study in piety, *Brainerd* strikes me as overly morose and inward.

That said, if one wants to engage Edwards, the Yale multivolume edition is the definitive place to go: *The Works of Jonathan Edwards*, vols. 1–26, ed. Perry Miller, John E. Smith, and Harry S. Stout (New Haven, CT: Yale University Press, 1956–2008). As I mentioned, the *Works of Jonathan Edwards Online* is an incredibly valuable resource. Not only are all the texts of the printed edition available electronically (fully searchable), but all the unpublished but transcribed materials are as well: http://edwards.yale.edu.

Books about Edwards

Now, as I have already noted, there are a lot of books on Edwards and more are produced every year (as is evidenced by the one you are holding right now). Beyond biography, there have been a number of extremely helpful books published about Edwards, ones that give insight, context, and understanding that are absolutely vital. To help sort through the chaff, I am going to give my top ten (well, actually eleven) books about Edwards that I have read, enjoyed, and profited by.

Stein, Stephen J., ed. *The Cambridge Companion to Jonathan Edwards*. New York: Cambridge University Press, 2007.

This is an extremely helpful book, as all *Cambridge Companion* volumes are. For one-stop shopping in current scholarship on Jonathan Edwards, this is the place to look. Nine of the essay authors edited volumes in the Yale edition; plus, the collection has contributions from Marsden and Gura, two recent biographers. There are essays that provide an understanding of local conditions and global challenges; the variety of roles Edwards played in his life (preacher, revivalist, theologian, philosopher, exegete, missionary); and his continuing legacy in American theology and culture.

Hatch, Nathan O., and Harry S. Stout, eds. *Jonathan Edwards and the American Experience*. New York: Oxford University Press, 1988.

Stein, Stephen J., ed. *Jonathan Edwards's Writings: Text, Context, Interpretation*. Bloomington: Indiana University Press, 1996.

Since we are talking about essay collections, these two are both valuable in drawing together new research on Jonathan Edwards. Both collections come from conferences on Jonathan Edwards sponsored by the Jonathan Edwards Center at Yale University. The first book, *Jonathan Edwards and the American Experience*, set the course of Edwards studies from the time of its publication in 1988. Norman Fiering's essay on Edwards's metaphysics, Stephen Stein's on Edwards as an exegete, and Mark Noll's on Edwards's continuing legacy in nineteenth-century theology—all were path-breaking at the time. The second book, *Jonathan Edwards's Writings*, focused especially on unpublished texts and unexplored contexts. The legacy section, which made up part three in the book, was especially provocative, containing revisionist understandings of Edwards's relationship with nineteenth-century theologians Nathaniel William Taylor, Charles Finney, and Edwards A. Park.

Cherry, Conrad. *The Theology of Jonathan Edwards: A Reappraisal*. 1966; repr., Bloomington: Indiana University Press, 1990.

This remains the finest single volume on Edwards's theology. Written in 1966 as a response to Perry Miller's approach of making the Puritan divine a spokesman for modern American thought and culture, Cherry rightly situates Edwards in the context of Puritan theology. Focusing on faith as an organizing center to Edwards's theology, Cherry demonstrates how faith intersects with covenant, justification, assurance, and perseverance. It still is the most satisfying explanation of large chunks of Edwards's theological program.

Pauw, Amy Plantinga. *The Supreme Harmony of All: The Trinitarian Theology of Jonathan Edwards*. Grand Rapids: Eerdmans, 2002.

Right behind Cherry's book in significance is Pauw's treatment of Edwards's Trinitarian theology. This book is both beautifully written and powerfully argued. Suggesting that Edwards functioned as "an ambidextrous theologian, who tailored a variety of rhetorical modes to specific polemical, pastoral, and intellectual contexts," Pauw reads Edwards's Trinitarianism in those terms—a cobbling together of various analogies in order to provide the ballast for his wide-ranging theological speculations. It should be obvious how much my accounting of Edwards's theology of the Christian life depends on Pauw's trendsetting work. I only wish I could write as graciously as she.

Lee, Sang Hyun. *The Philosophical Theology of Jonathan Edwards*. Princeton: Princeton University Press, 1988.

Lee's book is another that made a big impact on my understanding of Edwards. Vital are the ways in which Lee points up Edwards's new ontology, epistemology, and metaphysics. While I have to admit that much in this book was beyond my grasp on the first three readings (!), so much of what Lee suggests makes sense of large parts of Edwards's theological program. Particularly important is what Lee suggests about Edwards's use of disposition and habit, his understanding of knowledge and ways of knowing, and his commitment to beauty.

Brown, Robert E. *Jonathan Edwards and the Bible*. Bloomington: Indiana University Press, 2002.

When I read Brown's book in dissertation form, it blew me away. Here was an accounting of why Edwards focused on the historical mode, why he spent so much time in his later "Miscellanies" copying large swaths from universal histories, how he approached biblical texts, and what that final "divinity in an entire new method" could have looked like. The revised version published in 2002 was everything that the dissertation was, and more: a coherent, well-written, well-conceived understanding of Edwards's approach to biblical and historical criticism. Top-notch.

McDermott, Gerald R. *One Holy and Happy Society: The Public Theology of Jonathan Edwards*. University Park: Pennsylvania State University Press, 1992.

McDermott, Gerald R. *Jonathan Edwards Confronts the Gods: Christian Theology, Enlightenment Religion, and Non-Christian Faiths*. New York: Oxford University Press, 2000.

It is hard to imagine writing one significant book on Edwards, much less two. But my friend Gerald McDermott has. In the first book, which was his dissertation at the University of Iowa, McDermott shifts the conversation about Edwards. While in the past he was viewed as an "ivory tower" genius who was actually glad to slough off to Stockbridge where he wouldn't have to deal with his parishioners, McDermott presents a very different picture. His Edwards cared very much about the political and social fabric of Northampton and spent a great deal of time thinking, talking, and writing about it. In fact, Edwards was more tied into the politics of Northampton than may have been good for him; when his patron, Col. John Stoddard, died in 1748, suddenly he was at risk in ways that led to his dismissal two years later. The second book, *Jonathan Edwards Confronts the Gods*, is a learned work, one that situates Edwards within the context of the deist challenge and demonstrates how Edwards responded. Especially valuable are the chapters on how Edwards dealt with Judaism, Islam, Native Americans, and Chinese philosophers.

Tracy, Patricia J. *Jonathan Edwards, Pastor: Religion and Society in Eighteenth-Century Northampton*. New York: Hill and Wang, 1978.

While some might be put off by Tracy's tone, there is simply no other book that does what this one does. At the height of the historical profession's fascination with social history, Tracy produced a social history of Northampton during Edwards's ministry. The results are fascinating: statistical analysis about land ownership, generational transitions, ages of marriage, discipline and crime records—all tell something about Edwards's ministry. Thankfully, the book has been reprinted by Wipf and Stock in their Jonathan Edwards Classic Studies series. It is thought provoking and foundational.

Sweeney, Douglas A. *Jonathan Edwards and the Ministry of the Word: A Model of Faith and Thought.* Downers Grove, IL: InterVarsity, 2009.

This is an extremely valuable book by another friend of mine, Doug Sweeney, who teaches at Trinity Evangelical Divinity School. Part ministerial biography and part reflection on ministry, it is an accurate and accessible tour through Edwards's understanding of ministry. But in providing this, Doug also unpacks a great deal of Edwardsian theology. Extremely helpful.

Now, there are two other sets of books to mention. One set is of books written by my friend Stephen J. Nichols. Steve has produced a number of extremely valuable and accessible books on Edwards, all of which are worth reading: *Jonathan Edwards: A Guided Tour of His Life and Thought* (Phillipsburg, NJ: P&R, 2001); *An Absolute Sort of Certainty: The Holy Spirit and the Apologetics of Jonathan Edwards* (Phillipsburg, NJ: P&R, 2003); and *Heaven on Earth: Capturing Jonathan Edwards's Vision of Living in Between* (Wheaton, IL: Crossway, 2006). The first book is a helpful, brief introduction to Edwards's life and thought. Nichols does an excellent job explaining difficult and knotty Edwards writings—he helped me understand *Freedom of the Will.* The second was Steve's PhD dissertation from Westminster Seminary, but do not be frightened by that. It is an excellent introduction to how Edwards's views of epistemology shaped the way he engaged in apologetics. The third book is a retelling of Edwards's sermon "Heaven Is a World of Love," showing how it is necessary to be heavenly minded to be earthly good.

The other set of books to mention involves essays. Steve and I coedited a book, with D. G. Hart, that I would be remiss not to mention: D. G. Hart, Sean Michael Lucas, and Stephen J. Nichols, eds., *The Legacy of Jonathan Edwards: American Religion and the Evangelical Religion* (Grand Rapids: Baker, 2003). There are a number of valuable essays in that book, as evidenced in the notes to this project: Harry Stout on "Edwards' Tri-World Vision," George Marsden on the two dissertations, D. G. Hart on Edwards's connections with experiential Calvinism, and George Claghorn on his forty years of work in transcribing Edwards's letters. Another collection of essays worth mentioning is John Piper and Justin Taylor, eds., *A God-Entranced Vision of All Things: The Legacy of Jonathan Edwards* (Wheaton, IL: Crossway, 2004). These essays were originally presented at the 2003 Desiring God National Conference, and there were several important contributions: J. I. Packer on "the mind of Edwards"; Sherard Burns, an African American minister, on "trusting the theology of a slave owner"; and Paul Helm on Edwards's teaching on original sin.

These resources provide a starting point for exploring the life and thought of Jonathan Edwards. As that happens, I hope you keep in mind the most important thing: Edwards's desire for believers to see that they live in the midst of the history of the work of redemption. Through our union with Christ, we are participating in the uniting of all things in Christ; we are reflecting the divine glory back to the fountain of all good; we are looking for the coming of Christ's kingdom in its full and final form and the drawing up of earth into heaven. Do not miss that—it is God's grand design. May Edwards guide you more and more into seeing this divine design and your place in it.

APPENDIX 2

"A Man Just Like Us"

Jonathan Edwards and Spiritual Formation for Ministerial Candidates

Elijah was a man with a nature like ours, and he prayed fervently that it might not rain, and for three years and six months it did not rain on the earth. Then he prayed again, and heaven gave rain, and the earth bore its fruit. –James 5:17–18

It is hard for us to imagine, but there was a time when Jonathan Edwards was not "Jonathan Edwards." There was a time when Edwards was a Yale College student, preparing for ministry, and an inexperienced student supply for First Presbyterian Church, New York City. There was a time before the Great Awakening, *Religious Affections*, and *Freedom of the Will* made Edwards a household name in New England, when Edwards struggled to know God and to commune with God, to mortify his sins and to live for God's glory. As historian George M. Marsden put it in his recent biography of Edwards, "He was not a saint by nature. . . . His spiritual life was often an immense struggle. Despite his massive intellect and heroic disciplines, he was, like everyone else, a person with frailties and contradictions." In other words, Edwards was "a man just like one of us."[1]

To be sure, Edwards was well connected. After all, he was the son of Timothy Edwards, who pastored the church at East Windsor, Connecticut, for over sixty years, and the grandson of Solomon Stoddard, described as the "pope of the Connecticut Valley," who ruled the church of Northampton, Massachusetts, for fifty-seven years. Edwards would marry Sarah Pierpont, whose father was one of the leading figures of New England and a founder of New Haven, Connecticut. Edwards would receive one of the best educations that a colonialist could procure in those days, studying at Yale College, where he earned his AB and MA degrees and would serve as tutor in the dark days after the "Great Apostasy" of Yale rector Timothy Cutler and his tutors to Anglicanism in 1722. His family relations, his marriage, and his education all fitted him for leadership and, in this respect, probably set him apart from us.[2]

Yet, when we read the only records from his time as a student, supply pastor, and tutor, before he became "Jonathan Edwards," we find someone very much like us. In the "Resolutions," "Diary," "Miscellanies," and sermons from 1720 to 1723, we see a young man who wondered whether he would become holy in the midst of all his learning, whether his heart could and would stay inflamed with love to Christ as he lived with those so unlike himself. Even as a mature Edwards reflected back on these years in his "Personal

---

[1]George M. Marsden, *Jonathan Edwards: A Life* (New Haven, CT: Yale University Press, 2003), 1, 45, 50. For an overview of Edwards's spirituality, see Charles Hambrick-Stowe, "The 'Inward, Sweet Sense' of Christ in Jonathan Edwards," in *The Legacy of Jonathan Edwards: American Religion and the Evangelical Tradition*, ed. D. G. Hart, Sean Michael Lucas, and Stephen J. Nichols (Grand Rapids: Baker, 2003), 79–95.
[2]For a summary of these relations, see Kenneth Pieter Minkema, "The Edwardses: A Ministerial Family in Eighteenth Century New England," (PhD diss., University of Connecticut, 1988), esp. 148–205, and Marsden, *Jonathan Edwards*, 11–132.

Narrative," written for his son-in-law Aaron Burr Sr., around 1739 or 1740, he wondered at the wooing of the Spirit, rejoiced in his fervent love for Christ, and reminisced about his embrace of the sovereign Father. The trajectory of Edwards's future ministry began in those early years, when the "young Jonathan Edwards" pursued his ministerial training.[3]

Rather than offer a biographical sketch of these years in Edwards's life, which one can find in Marsden's encyclopedic biography, I would suggest that this period of Edwards's preparation provides a fruitful ground to gain insight into the whole process of spiritual formation for ministerial candidates. In both its positive and negative aspects, Edwards's spirituality during these years teaches important lessons about Reformed piety—how we as Christians and particularly as ministers of the gospel should live for God's glory. By considering Edwards's diary, resolutions, sermons, "Miscellanies," and other materials penned during the years at Yale, New York City, and Bolton, Connecticut, we will find encouragement for our souls, as well as possible difficulties with the introspective "Puritan conscience."[4] What then can be learned from Edwards as we seek to deepen our piety in preparation for future ministry?

Seek God and His Glorious Presence with Your Whole Being

If anything could be said about Edwards's approach to spirituality during his preparatory years, it would be that he sought God wholeheartedly. A good summary of Edwards's spirituality could be his diary entry from January 14, 1723: "Supposing there was never but one complete Christian, in all respects of a right stamp, having Christianity shining in its true luster, at a time in the world; resolved to act just as I would do, if I strove with all my might to be that one, that should be in my time." This entry recalls Edwards's

---

[3]William Sparkes Morris, *The Young Jonathan Edwards* (Brooklyn: Carlson, 1991); Jonathan Edwards, "Personal Narrative" in *The Works of Jonathan Edwards* (hereafter *WJE*), vol. 16, *Letters and Personal Writings*, ed. George S. Claghorn (New Haven, CT: Yale University Press, 1998), 799–800.

[4]Charles Lloyd Cohen, *God's Caress: The Psychology of Puritan Religious Experience* (New York: Oxford University Press, 1986); James Hoopes, "Calvinism and Consciousness from Edwards to Beecher," in *Jonathan Edwards and the American Experience*, ed. Nathan O. Hatch and Harry S. Stout (New York: Oxford University Press, 1988), 205–25.

famous resolutions, which expressed his Puritan determination to live every moment wholly for God. For example, Edwards "resolved, never to lose one moment of time; but improve it the most profitable way I possibly can"; "Resolved, to live with all my might, while I do live"; "Resolved, to endeavor to obtain for myself (as much happiness in the other world,) as I possibly can, with all the power, might, vigor, vehemence, yea violence, I am capable of, or can bring myself to exert, in any way that can be thought of"; and "Resolved, to strive to my utmost every week to be brought higher in religion, and to a higher exercise of grace, than I was the week before." Whatever else could be said about Edwards's spirituality, it was certainly intense.[5]

Perhaps Edwards believed that the Christian life demands such a wholehearted application because he was so aware of the deceitfulness of his own heart and the prevalence of his sins. Edwards saw his chief besetting sin to be pride. A mature Edwards later admitted, "I am greatly afflicted with a proud and self-righteous spirit; much more sensibly, than I used to be formerly. I see that serpent rising and putting forth its head, continually, everywhere, all around me." But even in his diary, recorded while he was supplying a Presbyterian church pulpit in New York, Edwards recognized his great battle with pride. "How hateful is a proud man!" he exclaimed. "How hateful is a worm that lifts up itself with pride! What a foolish, silly, miserable, blind, deceived, poor worm am I, when pride works!"[6]

Edwards's proud spirit manifested itself primarily in argument with others. He recognized that he had "a certain inclination" to "too much dogmaticalness, too much of the egotism." This dogmatic spirit apparently led to sins of anger and rash speech. In one diary entry, on July 1, 1723, Edwards "resolved for the future to observe rather more of meekness, moderation, and temper in disputes." Three days later, he made the same resolution, perhaps reflecting the difficulty he was having with controlling his words. Two weeks after this, on July 18, 1723, Edwards records,

---

[5] "Diary," January 14, 1723, in *WJE*, 16:764; Resolutions no. 5, 6, 7, 22, 30, in *WJE*, 16:753–55.

[6] "Personal Narrative," *WJE*, 16:803; "Diary," March 2, 1723, *WJE*, 16:767.

"Resolved to endeavor to make sure of that sign the apostle James gives of a perfect man, Jas. 3:2, 'If any man offend not in word, the same is a perfect man, and able also to bridle the whole body.'" A month later, Edwards advised himself that there ought to "be something of benevolence in all that I speak," evidence that his pride was still being pricked and evidenced by his speech. Still later, Edwards counseled himself that "there is much folly when I am quite sure I am in the right, and others are positive in contradicting me, to enter into a vehement or long debate upon it."[7]

As Edwards warred against these sins, he sought God with his entire being. He craved the "inward, sweet delight in God and divine things" that he had experienced around 1721, a year after he graduated from Yale. Edwards continued to immerse himself in Scripture, in which he had "the greatest delight." Edwards later observed that during these years as a ministerial candidate,

> oftentimes in reading [Scripture], every word seemed to touch my heart. I felt an harmony between something in my heart, and those sweet and powerful words. I seemed often to see so much light, exhibited by every sentence, and such a refreshing ravishing food communicated, that I could not get along in reading.

His view of God expanded as he began to delight in the nature and character of God. He gained

> a sweet sense of the glorious majesty and grace of God, that I know not how to express. I seemed to see them both in a sweet conjunction: majesty and meekness joined together: it was a sweet and gentle, and holy majesty; and also a majestic meekness; and awful sweetness; a high, and great, and holy gentleness.

The result was that Edwards had a profound, whole-souled longing to enjoy God's presence and to commune with him. He described it

---

[7]All quotations from "Diary," *WJE*, 16: May 4, 1723 (769); July 1, 1723 (773); July 4, 1723; July 18, 1723; and July 20, 1723 (774–75); August 17, 1723 (779); September 2, 1723 (781). See also diary entries for May 22 and 27, 1723 (771); December 12, 1723 (782); December 31, 1723 (783).

as "a sweet burning in my heart; an ardor of my soul, that I know not how to express." But this longing for God's presence connected with a passionate desire for holiness. "I felt in me a burning desire to be in everything a complete Christian; and conformed to the blessed image of Christ: and that I might live, in all things, according to the pure, sweet, and blessed rules of the gospel." He went on to observe that "it was my continual strife day and night, and constant inquiry, how I should be more holy, and live more holily, and more becoming a child of God, and disciple of Christ."[8] For Edwards, who struggled with pride, angry words, and a dogmatic spirit, the holiness that he sought with his whole being appeared to be quite contrary and almost unattainable. Yet he sought it with his whole being because he believed that without holiness, one could not and would not see God and know his presence.[9]

Understand that You Belong Completely to God

While Edwards was serving the Presbyterian church in New York, he underwent a solemn renewal of the promises made for him in baptism when he was an infant. In this renewal, written in his diary, he reaffirmed, "I . . . have given myself, all that I am and have to God, so that I am not in any respect my own." This utter dedication to God involved every facet of Edwards's being.

> I can challenge no right in this understanding, this will, these affections that are in me; neither have I any right to this body, or any of its members: no right to this tongue, these hands, nor feet; no right to these senses, these eyes, these ears, this smell or taste. I have given myself clear away, and have not retained anything as my own. I have been to God this morning and told him that I gave myself *wholly* to him.[10]

---

[8] "Personal Narrative," *WJE*, 16:792, 793, 795, 797.
[9] Jonathan Edwards, "The Way of Holiness," in *WJE*, vol. 10, *Sermons and Discourses, 1720–1723*, ed. Wilson H. Kimnach (New Haven, CT: Yale University Press, 1992), 471–73, 478–79. The last paragraph of this sermon was almost a verbatim transcription of his first entry in his "Miscellanies"; see "The 'Miscellanies,' a," in *WJE*, vol. 13, *The "Miscellanies," a–500*, ed. Thomas A. Schafer (New Haven, CT: Yale University Press, 1994), 163–64.
[10] "Diary," January 12, 1723, *WJE*, 16:762.

This time of self-dedication to God obviously made an impression on Edwards. Around this same period, Edwards preached a sermon to his New York City congregation on "dedication to God." He held that "offering up ourselves to God" is the "greatest of all the duties of a Christian." In this, Edwards believed the Christian makes "an absolute renunciation of the world," "a joyful receiving of God as our whole portion and happiness," "a willing embracing all his commands," and "a resignation to his will." Believers have to make this offering to God because he is their Creator, Sustainer, and Redeemer. As a result, he is an absolute sovereign who demands total obedience. Further, believers have to "stand" to their baptism by giving themselves up completely to God's service. The only other choice is to renounce one's baptism "and turn atheists or heathen." Finally, Edwards's most compelling reason for dedication to God was that "if you give yourself to God, he will also give himself to you. You give yourself to him to be his servant; he will give himself to you to be your portion and everlasting happiness, and thereby you are sure of eternal glory, because the infinite source and fountain of eternal glory is yours already."[11]

This understanding that we belong wholly to God provided Edwards with a firm grounding for certainty and assurance. At one point in his sermon, he proclaimed that if his listeners were wholly given to God,

> You may [be] certain of his love and favor, certain of his guidance in all your ways, certain that no evil shall befall you, certain that whatever befalls you is for your good; for you know and are certain that you are God's for you have given yourself to him, and therefore you are certain that he will do by you in all respects as to one that is his.

This confidence that Edwards knew bears an important resemblance to one of the Reformed tradition's classic statements of belonging to God. The first answer of the Heidelberg Catechism claims that a Christian's only comfort in life and death is "that

---

[11] "Dedication to God," in *WJE*, 10:551, 553, 555–57, 559.

I am not my own, but belong—body and soul, in life and in death—to my faithful Savior Jesus Christ." This belonging to God in Christ is rooted in the reality of the atonement and the continuance of divine providence. As a result of this belonging, "Christ, by his Holy Spirit, assures me of eternal life and makes me wholeheartedly willing and ready from now on to live for him." For those preparing for ministry, this confidence that God in Christ is working all things together for our salvation will enable us to "lie and rest quietly and securely in the midst of storms and tempests, fearing nothing, knowing that [we] are in God's hands where nothing can hurt [us]."[12]

Remember that Holiness Is by Grace

With all of his "violent" striving for holiness, Edwards sometimes seemed to exemplify the temptation to gain holiness by works, rather than by grace. His diary was filled with reproachful reminders that his spiritual condition depended upon self-denial in eating, drinking, and sleeping; that he was not properly using his time for God's glory; and that he needed to devote even more time to private prayer. As he focused on these exercises of self-denial and turned his gaze inward, his religious feelings ebbed and flowed. Over a two-week period at the end of 1722, his spirituality ran the gamut: on December 21, "This day, and yesterday, I was exceedingly dull, dry, and dead"; the next day, he reported, "This day revived by God's Spirit"; by December 24 he had "higher thoughts than usual of the excellency of Jesus Christ and his kingdom," only to return "dull and lifeless" on December 29 and to experience dullness on both January 1 and 2. Such reporting went on throughout his diary, marking his spiritual temperature. By engaging in this introspective spirituality at this point in his life, Edwards seemed to conflate his wholehearted pursuit of God's glory with right standing with God.[13]

---

[12]Ibid., 10:558; Heidelberg Catechism, Q. 1, in *Ecumenical Creeds and Reformed Confessions* (Grand Rapids: Christian Reformed Church, 1988), 13.
[13]"Diary," December 21, 1722; December 22, 1722; December 24, 1722; December 29, 1722; January 1, 1723; January 2, 1723, all found in *WJE*, 16:759–60. Edwards

To be fair, at his best moments (or moments of frustration with his rigorous spiritual practice) Edwards recognized that his sanctification would progress only through the work of the Holy Spirit. At around the same time that Edwards renewed his baptismal covenant and gave himself anew to God, he also confessed in his diary, "I find by experience, that let me make resolutions, and do what I will, with never so many inventions, it is all nothing, and to no purpose at all, without the motions of the Spirit of God." In his pursuit of God's glory, through his self-examinations and strict resolution, Edwards realized that "it is to no purpose to resolve, except we depend on the grace of God; for if it were not for his mere grace, one might be a very good man one day, and a very wicked one the next." In a later meditation, Edwards reveled in the work of God's gracious Spirit: "Felt the doctrines of election, free grace, and of our not being able to do anything without the grace of God; and that holiness is entirely, throughout, the work of God's Spirit, with more pleasure than before."[14]

In addition, Edwards would later recognize that his constant self-examinations and scheming for holiness occurred "with too great a dependence on my own strength; which afterwards proved a great damage to me." As he continued on in the Christian life, he learned two things: "my extreme feebleness and impotence, every manner of way; and the innumerable and bottomless depths of secret corruption and deceit, that there was in my heart." The only true solution to the intractable problem of human depravity would not be self-willed striving, but "a more full and constant sense of the absolute sovereignty of God, and a delight in that sovereignty . . . [and] more of a sense of the glory of Christ, as a mediator, as revealed in the gospel." If Edwards was to make any progress in the Christian life, it would be solely because of the sovereign work of God's Spirit motivated by God's amazing grace and rooted in God's glorious gospel.[15]

---

would counsel his New York City auditors on the "duty of self-examination," in *WJE*, 10:482–92.

[14] "Diary," January 2, 1723, *WJE*, 16:760; "Diary," March 6, 1723, *WJE*, 16:767.

[15] "Personal Narrative," *WJE*, 16:795, 803.

The Chief Fruit of Spiritual Grace Is Love for God and Others

In the end, Edwards's spirituality focused on love for God and others as the chief mark of the Christian life. Looking back on these years of preparation, he observed that he spent much of his time meditating on heaven because it appeared to be "a great part of the happiness of heaven, that there the saints could express their love to Christ." Edwards felt frustration that he could not fully express his love for God as he desired. "The inward ardor of my soul," he noted,

> seemed to be hindered and pent up, and could not freely flame out as it would. I used often to think, how in heaven, this sweet principle should freely and fully vent and express itself. Heaven appeared to me exceeding delightful as a world of love. It appeared to me, that all happiness consisted in living in pure, humble, heavenly, divine love.[16]

As a supply preacher in New York, Edwards preached two sermons that sought to put this love into language. In one sermon, Edwards tried to persuade his congregation to give themselves in love to Christ. The chief motivation to do so was "the loveliness of Christ" himself. Meditating on the ways in which Christ was like the rose of Sharon, he proclaimed:

> Here, O believers, O lovers of Christ, is a rose for you, to be ravished with the fragrance of it, for your eyes to be delighted with the infinite beauty of, for you to be delighted to all eternity in the enjoyment of. This rose and lily is the brightness of God's glory and the express image of his person, which is so amiable and fragrant that it is the eternal and infinite delight of the Father himself.

Unlike human loves that can be alloyed with impure motives or faulty objects, "the love of Christ is the love of that which is truly above all things excellent and lovely, and therefore the pleasures that result from it must be solid, real, substantial, and never fad-

---

[16]Ibid., 795–96.

ing." Only by giving oneself in love to Jesus Christ does one experience a union "more intimate than between any other lovers."[17] Toward the end of his ministry in New York, Edwards preached another sermon on "true love to God." Arguing that "true love to God makes the duties he requires of us easy and delightful," Edwards taught that "the soul, having had a discovery of the glories of God made to it and being ravished thereby, is transformed into the same image from glory to glory, so that he may see the image of those beloved beauties and excellencies reflected on himself." As the soul experiences divine transformation by meditative love for God's beauty, it discovers that the pleasures of love for God are "greater and better than any sensual delights." Such love keeps believers from sin and motivates them to greater and higher service.[18]

Importantly, in light of the sins with which Edwards struggled, love for God manifests itself in character qualities toward others such as humility and gentleness. Edwards certainly longed for humility to replace his pride, and he talked about that virtue in terms that paralleled his discussion of love. "How immensely more pleasant is an humble delight, than a high thought of myself!" Edwards exclaimed in his diary. "O, how much more pleasanter is humility than pride! O, that God would fill me with exceeding great humility, and that he would evermore keep me from all pride! The pleasures of humility are really the most refined, inward and exquisite delights in the world." Likewise, Edwards esteemed gentleness as a character trait that others would see. He lamented in his diary that "a virtue, which I need in a higher degree, to give a beauty and luster to my behavior is gentleness. If I had more of an air of gentleness, I should be much mended."[19]

Edwards viewed humility and gentleness, two virtues that he felt he lacked, to be the chief indicators of genuine love for God and others. In 1738, as he preached his sermon series on 1 Corin-

---

[17] "Fragment: Application on Love to Christ," in *WJE*, 10:612–13, 615, 617.
[18] "True Love to God," in *WJE*, 10:636, 638, 641. A section of this sermon incorporated material from the "Miscellanies" no. x, written about this time (cf. p. 642 with *WJE*, 13:175–76). By looking at the "Miscellanies," one may find that Edwards also meditated on union with Christ and God's love for believers during this time.
[19] "Diary," March 2, 1723, *WJE*, 16:767; "Diary," February 16, 1725, *WJE*, 16:787.

thians 13 to his congregation at Northampton, he argued that "the spirit of Christian love is opposite to a proud behavior." Indeed, "true divine love is an humble love." Once one discovers the loveliness and beauty of God, he cannot help but be humbled before God and others. "If the knowledge of God as lovely causes humility, then a respect to God as lovely implies humility. And from this love to God arises a Christian love to men," Edwards claimed. In addition, genuine love for God and others produces an abhorrence of sin, which leads believers to pursue holiness, connecting love for God, holiness, and humility. But genuine love for God also produces gentleness in dealing with others. In his "Charity and Its Fruits" sermons, Edwards stated that gentleness is a subset of the long-suffering that a loving spirit produces. Here again, love, humility, and gentleness are tied together in Edwards's view: "Humility is a main root of a meek and long-suffering spirit, because it makes him less disposed to a high resentment of injuries. . . . It is pride which is very much the foundation of high and bitter resentment and revengeful spirit." Love, the chief spiritual grace, produces an invigorated love for God and a humbled love for others.[20]

Edwards never deviated from this basic approach to spiritual formation, which he developed in his years of ministerial preparation. In fact, his preaching in Northampton; his writing during the Great Awakening, preeminently *Religious Affections* and *Charity and Its Fruits*; and his dissertation *The Nature of True Virtue* echo many of these themes. Those of us seeking to serve as pastors in Christ's church can learn important lessons from this man, Jonathan Edwards, because he was just like one of us. May God grant that our heartbeat would become more like his. Those who seek the presence of God must offer themselves wholeheartedly to God out of a passionate love for God and others, the evidence of which will be a humble reliance upon God's sovereign grace and a gentle spirit with God's people.

---

[20]Jonathan Edwards, "Charity and Its Fruits," in *WJE*, vol. 8, *Ethical Writings*, ed. Paul Ramsey (New Haven, CT: Yale University Press, 1989), 194, 233, 243, 245–46. Edwards also discussed humility and gentleness as the sixth sign in *Religious Affections*; see *WJE*, vol. 2, *Religious Affections*, ed. John E. Smith (New Haven, CT: Yale University Press, 1959), 311–40.

Index